B.U.D.
Better, Unique, & Desirable:
The Sales Process That Gets
Results

By Thomas Ellis

Twin Horseshoes Publishing
www.twinhorseshoes.ca
Ontario, Canada

Ellis, Thomas
B.U.D. Better, Unique, & Desirable: The Sales Process That Gets Results

eBook ISBN 978-0-578-35100-1
Paperback ISBN 978-0-578-35099-8

Nonfiction | Business & Economics | Development | Business Development
Nonfiction | Business & Economics | Sales & Selling | General
Nonfiction | Business & Economics | Personal Success

DEDICATION

To my son Thomas – Thank you for allowing me to be more than just your Dad.

TABLE OF CONTENTS

FOREWORD

I first met Thomas Ellis when he started attending Institute for Excellence in Sales (IES) programs, and I was immediately impressed by his presence and ability to make all the people around him feel comfortable, important, and valued. We were honored to bestow our 2017 IES Member of the Year award to him as he became a welcomed ambassador in our organization.

A career in sales is hard. It's a tough profession and to be successful, you need to keep learning, honing your skills, and creating value for your customers and prospects. Not everyone will be successful. Even those who are successful will encounter difficulty along the way as the market shifts, customers evolve, and competitors emerge. So, how do you become Better, Unique, and Desirable?

To truly become a sales professional, you need to continuously develop your sales skills. The same way a professional athlete needs to train, develop their mindset, and get stronger, sales professionals need to learn how to prepare, present more effectively, and build networks. Thomas spells out how they can continue to do so while becoming better, unique, and more desirable.

As the cofounder of the Institute for Excellence in Sales, a global organization for sales leaders and their teams, I am privileged to meet sales experts around globe, such as Thomas, and often invite them to participate in our programs. I am thrilled that Thomas has put his best practices into this book so that thousands of other sales professionals can take their career to the next level and get better, unique, and more desirable.

Enjoy the book!

Fred Diamond
Institute for Excellence in Sales
Award-Winning Sales Game Changers Webcasts and
Podcasts
Fairfax, VA

INTRODUCTION

The culture of sales has changed in the last century. We live in the information age where businesses and consumers alike can access information with the click of their mouse. What does this mean for the modern sales representative?

It means that antiquated sales methods no longer work with today's buyer. Before the information age, sales reps had a degree of power in the salesperson/buyer relationship because they had something the buyer needed and all of the information they wanted, they had to get directly from the sales representative. That is no longer the case. Today, we face educated buyers that have done their due diligence way before you contact them for the first time.

As a result, today's sales rep must be informed and ready to provide a unique selling proposition that will leverage their relationship with their buyer to create a sale. Different characteristics enable today's sales professionals to be more effective. In this book, we will review those characteristics along with specific tips to help sales reps leverage their success throughout the sales process.

CHAPTER 1: THE B.U.D. FACTOR

Over my years of experience, I've developed my own sales philosophy that I like to employ throughout the sales process. That philosophy is called the B.U.D. Factor and it stands for Better, Unique, and Desirable. This process was actually part of my inspiration for creating this book.

I'd like to share with you how this process can impact your sales and set you up for success. The B.U.D. factor represents characteristics you need to embody to serve your customer and ultimately close more sales.

BETTER

How do you become better in the sales process? First, it is important to acknowledge what it means to be better. The dictionary defines better as "excellent or effective type of quality." To be better, you must strive to do what others aren't willing to do.

How do you step up and become better than your peers and competition?

It sounds simple but, you must be prepared! We discussed this a bit already, but it bears repeating because proper preparation is not a quality many salespeople possess. That is why those who employ these characteristics, rise above the crowd to become the best of their profession.

Adequate preparation doesn't just make you more efficient as a salesperson, but it shows your customer or prospect that you respect their time. Time is one of our most precious commodities and once it's gone, you can never get it back. Therefore, it is imperative that you are always cognizant of the time you are taking when you schedule a call or an appointment with a customer or prospect. If you tell them you will only need 10 minutes of their time, stick to that schedule. Prepare in advance of this call to ensure you cover what you intend and manage the customer or prospect's expectations appropriately. If you are setting up a call or meeting with the customer, set their expectations and let them know what will be covered in the meeting; that way, when you connect, there are no surprises. The prospect will know exactly what to expect when they meet with or talk to you. When they see that you respect their time and their schedule, you will, in turn, gain their respect and trust.

When running a meeting with a prospect, part of your preparation is to conduct research on the company prior to your meeting. Few salespeople prepare for a sales meeting to this level of detail. Take the time to review their website and learn more about what they do. Look them up on social media. Gain as much information about them as you can so that you can go into the meeting armed with information about their business and how they run. When you attend the meeting and show that you've done your homework, you will not only impress your prospect, but you will show them that you are serious about partnering and doing business with them. If this doesn't make you BETTER than the competition, I don't know what will.

Part of your preparation will also include preparation for objections. You will not go through a sales process without objections. Anticipate those objections and prepare for them in advance.

Finally, be prepared to demonstrate to your prospect why your product or service is a good fit for them. This is where some of your homework on the company will come in handy. There was probably a reason why this prospect came to you as a target or a referral. Focus on specific characteristics about their company that fit perfectly with your product or service. Combine this with questions they may have already answered about their specific operation to suggest the best solution for them.

Most salespeople will exercise aspects of this level of preparation, but few will incorporate all of them. That is what will make you BETTER.

UNIQUE

People are drawn to things that are unique. When it comes to sales, you should have a USP, a unique selling proposition. Your unique selling proposition represents what it is that you do that stands out from everyone else. How do you differ from your competition? You should be able to clearly identify what your USP is for your business or the company that you work for, but what about your personal USP?

People buy YOU before they buy your products or services. What is it about you that is attracting your prospects to you? Why do they want to buy from you? This will be your personal USP. As you are in the process of developing your personal USP, here are some simple suggestions to make you stand out among your prospects and customers:

- ***Send a personal handwritten thank you note.*** This is a lost art these days. We live in an electronic world where it's so much easier to send an email, an eCard or use social media to connect with someone and thank them. While these methods are all great, nothing can replace the effect of receiving a personalized handwritten note. It shows your prospect or customer that you care enough to take the time to write them a handwritten note. Send a handwritten note to your prospect after your next sales meeting. Watch the impression it makes.

- ***Send an article of interest to your prospect or customer.*** Remember when we talked about doing your homework before your meeting with a customer? After taking the time to do your homework on their business, subscribe to some trade magazines or an email list to stay up to date on things happening in their industry. If you notice something of interest, send it to them. It will show your prospect that you are in tune with their business and their interests.

- ***Connect with your prospect via social media.*** Use the power of social media to connect with your prospect prior to a meeting. Use this platform to start building a relationship with your prospect before you meet with them. Study their profile, posts and interests and create a level of engagement between them to facilitate a relationship. This will be the first level of research you will conduct with them as you learn more about their business and their needs.

- ***Send a meeting agenda prior to your meeting with your prospect.*** Sending your prospect an agenda prior to your meeting shows another level of preparation. When we discussed better, we talked about respecting your client's time by being prepared. This is another demonstration of that. Few salespeople focus on the prospect and their needs when setting a meeting; most are just focused on accomplishing their own agenda. By being prepared, you are keeping the focus on them and their needs.

DESIRABLE

I touched on this earlier, but people do business with people they like. To stand above the competition and create sales success, you must be desirable to your prospects and customers. You must create an environment where they want to do business with you. One way to do this is through your USP which we touched on when we were talking about what makes you unique.

Here are some suggestions of how to make yourself desirable to your prospects and customers:

- *Under promise and over deliver.* Most salespeople are notorious for doing this backwards. They over promise and under deliver. It's never intentional; they must be ambitious about getting the business and end up setting unrealistic goals for the client which sets improper expectations in the beginning of the relationship and compromises the business. Even if the customer asks for something you want to be able to give to them, but you are not sure you'll be able to deliver, be candid with them and tell them it is something you might not be able to do. They will respect your honesty, and if you are able to make it happen, it will be a pleasant surprise for them. Continue to give them pleasant surprises.

- ***Always do what you say you're going to do.*** Your prospect or customer needs to know that you are reliable and good for your word. This starts early in the sales process. For example, if your sales meeting is set for 10:00, don't arrive at 10:05 and think it's no big deal because it is just 5 minutes. First, it shows lack of respect for your client's time, even if it's just 5 minutes. Second, you are not showing that you are good for your word early in the process, failing to make a good impression. If you say you're going to be there at 10:00, be there at 9:55. I understand that sometimes things can come up that we cannot always control, but part of being prepared means allotting extra time in your schedule to consider unforeseen circumstances like traffic. Be mindful of what you say to your prospect or client and be good for your word.

- ***Sell the customer what THEY want, not what you want them to buy.*** Just because your boss is running an incentive on a particular product or service this month doesn't mean it is the best fit for your prospect. This is why active listening is so important. If you just take the time to listen to your prospect, they will always tell you exactly what they need. Ask qualifying questions for clarity but let the answer come from them, not you. You are there as a guide only.

- ***You help the customer buy; you don't sell.*** This is a difficult concept for some salespeople to get; you're in sales after all. The hard truth is no one wants to be sold. Prospects are more likely to commit to purchase when they feel like the choice was their idea. Your job is to provide information, serve as a professional expert on the product or service and advise them through the process. When the prospect feels as if they are partnering with you as an advisor, they are more likely to make a buying decision. They don't need to be convinced or sold anything. You don't need to be aggressive. Just provide them with the information they need and allow them to make the decision. Don't play into the negative sales stereotypes. You are not the used car salesperson.

Better, Unique, Desirable: It's a simple sales philosophy that I weave throughout my sales process to create a path to success. Use these characteristics to elevate your sales and take into consideration as we continue to walk through each sales component to create the results you desire.

ARE YOU B.U.D.?

BETTER: *Are you standing out among your peers and competitors? What is your unique advantage? Are you willing to do what others won't just to be better?*

UNIQUE: *Identify your USP, unique selling proposition. This is your secret sauce that will set you apart from others. Start by implementing simple strategies like sending handwritten thank you notes to your prospects.*

DESIRABLE: *Create an environment where your prospects want to do business with you. What characteristics do you embody that will attract them to you rather than repel?*

CASE STUDY: B.U.D.

VINCE

I met Vince at the Institute for Excellence in Sales. After getting to know each other, I learned that he had a need for guidance in leading and driving results with his sales team. He had a specific desire to train his new sales representatives and develop a plan to get them up to speed and productive quickly.

Vince sought my assistance in teaching the fundamentals of sales to his team. To quote Vince who likes to use sport analogies, "to play good football, you have to block and tackle." He wanted to implement this train of thought with his team. Vince appreciated my approach of breaking sales down into small bite-sized pieces that his team could digest. I understand that too much information results in overload and a team that is lack luster and unmotivated. When you are able to teach in small chunks that the team can digest, it allows them to celebrate small successes along the way, showing them visible progress on their journey. The reality is sales is not complicated. It really is quite simple, but simple does not equate to easy.

Vince and his team really latched on to my B.U.D. and prospecting strategy to build their sales. Even the senior sales representatives were able to learn something to improve their strategy after my training session. The team was very receptive, and they found my approach to align directly with their needs.

The result of my training was an increase in performance among the junior sales representatives, along with the adaptation of new skill sets to put to use in their daily sales habits.

CHAPTER 2: ARE YOU EXCITED ABOUT WHAT YOU'RE DOING?

Before we start discussing the mindset of sales and how it affects your ability to perform, we must first analyze where your passion lies. In my experience, you will not build a successful sales career, or any career for that matter, without passion.

Merriam-Webster defines passion as "a strong feeling of enthusiasm or excitement for something or about doing something" (Merriam-Webster, n.d.) Do you feel that way about your job? If not, is there anything you can do to ignite that spark? Think back to when you first applied for your current sales job. What attracted you to it? Why were you excited about the prospect of working for that company? If that spark has faded, since you've been with the company, you need to evaluate whether or not you can get it back. Without passion, your productivity and results will fade. Sales thrives on passion. It is not a job that you can just place on autopilot and expect results to come. It requires work – work to build relationships, work to close sales and work to develop yourself. Without these components, you are setting yourself up for failure.

Passion is the energy force that will fuel your discipline to get the job done each day. There are going to be aspects of your job that you don't like as much. That's okay. It doesn't mean you're not passionate about your job. Your passion will push you to do the things you don't always want to do because of your anticipated outcome. Ask yourself why you are doing what you're doing. Is it because you enjoy working with people and building relationships? Take it a step further and ask yourself how much you believe in the product you're selling. Do you think it can truly help your customers and improve their way of life or their business? If so, you might be on the right track for discovering your passion for your occupation and the company you work for. You may be wondering why we are focusing on this when this book is designed to teach you how to become a better salesperson. We are focusing on this first because passion is the foundation on which you will build your successful sales career. Without it, your structure will crumble. For all of the principles that we will discuss in the book to take root, you need to understand and commit to being passionate about what you do.

Whenever you run into problems hitting your goals or you feel stuck in your sales job, the first thing I encourage you to do is check your passion meter. How are you feeling about what you're doing? Has something changed? If something has changed, identify what that is so that you can deal with it. It could be something as simple as a company policy that has changed, and you feel it is making it more difficult for you to connect with your customer. If you truly enjoy what you do and still believe in the product you're selling, you can find a way to work around this change. In such a case, I'd also encourage you to talk to your sales manager and brainstorm ways for you to work around this issue so that you can get excited about your work again.

If you're relatively new at your job and your passion is lacking because you feel inferior as a novice, re-evaluate why you took this job in the first place. It takes time to learn product knowledge and adjust to a new company. Don't get caught up in the minutia. Instead, embrace your passion and you will attract people to you. As you meet with new prospects, they will be attracted to your passion and enthusiasm, even if you don't have all of the answers. No one has all of the answers; just be willing to go get them.

Passion combined with qualities like drive, focus, commitment, and integrity will amplify your results as a sales professional.

DRIVE

When you're passionate about what you do, it feeds your drive to succeed. What drives you? A driven sales professional doesn't need to have their hand held; they're anxious to get out there and create results. With the appropriate drive, you must be humble enough to accept direction and leadership as you need it, but autonomous enough to stand on your own without any prodding. A passionate sales professional with drive doesn't sit at their desk every day waiting for 5:00 pm. Instead, they are focused on what they can get done each day, no matter how long it takes. Do you feel this way about your career? If not, what would it take to increase your drive?

FOCUS

Passionate salespeople are laser focused. They identify their goals or targets, and they develop a strategy to achieve those goals, without distraction. They are committed to meeting the needs of their clients or prospects, providing solutions that will improve their quality of life or business. When you are a passionate sales professional that is focused on your craft, excellence is part of your philosophy. You will not allow anything to derail you from moving forward in achieving your goals. How focused are you as a sales professional? If this is a point of weakness, or are you committed to developing your focus to improve and grow?

COMMITMENT

Passion solidifies your commitment. When you are passionate, you are willing to do whatever it takes to get the job done. In sales, your commitment spans beyond just the company you work for; you are committed to your career. That being said, you will not quit easily. The fact that you picked up this book is a sign of your passion and commitment to your career. If you're feeling stuck or you just want to improve as a sales professional, that is a sign of commitment and pride in what you do. That all stems from your passion.

INTEGRITY

Integrity is a sign of your character and who you are. All sales professionals should embody this trait. Integrity is who you are when no one's looking. If your behavior and activity is one way when the boss is watching and another way when you're alone, you are not acting in integrity. When you are passionate about your career, you don't need anyone watching over your shoulder to make sure you're doing your job right; you possess the desire within you to always want to do the job correctly.

All of these characteristics properly weaved together will fuel your passion for your sales career. Before we dive into techniques and strategies to make you a successful sales professional, start by asking yourself the question, am I passionate about what I do? Think about why you do what you do. Every sales professional has a different story in how they got started. Many stumbled into this career which is not necessarily a bad thing. If you chose to stay in sales, ask yourself why? Why do you love sales? What has kept you in this field for so long? If you've been struggling in your career lately, ask yourself why? Have some of the elements that fueled your passion been taken away? If so, ask yourself if this is something that can be fixed, whether it is in your current role or a new one. Before you read on, make sure sales is something you are still passionate about. Even if that passion is dormant, it can still be awakened with the right action and motivation.

B.U.D. STRATEGY FOR BEING A PASSIONATE SALES PROFESSIONAL

BETTER: Channel your excitement and find your why. If you don't know why you're doing what you're doing, you'll never develop an excitement about doing it.

UNIQUE: Integrate your passion and strength into how you can best serve your prospect and customer. Allow it to fuel your creativity.

DESIRABLE: Passion is magnetic. Attract people to you through your excitement and commitment to what you're doing.

CHAPTER 3: MINDSET

Now that we've arranged the foundation by identifying what you're passionate about, we can start to build the frame of your sales career. Building a successful sales career doesn't start with setting the appointment. It doesn't even start with closing the sale. Before you are able to do either of those things, you must adjust your mindset to build the appropriate habits that will drive you toward success.

Good habits will move you forward to reaching your goals and hitting all of your targets. Bad habits will hold you back and keep you stagnant. The problem is many sales professionals don't even realize or acknowledge their bad habits and that keeps them stuck. Let's examine the power of establishing good or bad habits.

As children, one of the first habits you probably remember learning is brushing your teeth. As a kid, your parents often had to remind you to brush your teeth because the habit was still new, but as an adult, does anyone have to tell you to brush your teeth anymore? Of course not. It's muscle memory, a habit that you've built over a period of years. Conversely, as a child you may have developed a habit of eating sugary snacks and that habit has followed you into adulthood. As a result, you may have had many visits to the dentist for cavities, the price for your sugary snacks. When it comes to bad habits, many people don't realize the damage they are doing until consequences appear. In the case of sugary snacks, it's a cavity. In the case of sales, it's lower performance and less sales. The problem is, in sales, we become comfortable making excuses for our bad habits.

DON'T MAKE EXCUSES

One bad habit that holds many sales professionals back is making excuses.

The competition is too stiff.
Our prices are too high.
I'm too new at this.
My dog got sick this morning.

Excuses do nothing to move you toward your goal, and they are often a disguise for an insecurity or deficiency in your process. They keep you stuck. Take responsibility. Own your situation. If you suck at prospecting, admit it. That is the only way you are going to tackle the problem and master it. There is nothing wrong with failure as long as you are willing to learn from it. There is, however, something wrong with hiding behind your excuses and using that as a crutch to explain why you are not moving forward.

YOU DON'T HAVE TO KNOW IT ALL

As a sales professional, it is your job to leverage yourself as an expert in your field, but that does not mean that you have to know everything. The enemy of good is great. While some may believe perfectionism is a good trait, it is not. It will keep you stuck focusing on things that will not move you forward. If you feel like you have to know everything before being able to serve your customer, how much time are you losing in reaching your sales goal? Perfectionism is a crutch. Let it go. Even worse, claiming to be a 'know it all' when you don't will likely damage your relationship with your potential prospect or customer. They will respect you much more if you are willing to admit when you don't know all of the answers. Just be diligent in finding the answers for them when you don't know them, and you'll be well on your way to a good, honest relationship with your customer.

AVOID DISTRACTIONS

In the last chapter, we mentioned focus as a key element of fueling your passion. The opposite of focus is distractions. With so many things competing for our attention these days, it is easy to allow distractions like emails and pings from our phone to take away from our focus on the prospect or customer. If you know you have a problem with distractions, turn these things off. When you are meeting with or talking to a prospect or customer, your attention should be 100% on them. Stay focused and listen actively to what they are saying.

Adjusting your mindset, beginning with strong daily habits will construct the framework of a successful sales career.

What exactly are good sales habits?

ACTIVE LISTENER

Great sales professionals know how to listen. It's not the dog and pony show that so many people refer to when you meet with the customer. When you meet with your customer or prospect, the spotlight should be on them and you're holding the mic.

PROACTIVE PLANNING

Great sales professionals are proactive rather than reactive. You don't have to let a situation control you. Rather, you can plan properly and control the process yourself. A great sales professional knows how to smoothly guide their prospects through their sales process seamlessly. This is done by proper planning which includes but is not limited to studying your prospects and their needs and the best solutions. Get into the habit of being proactive by planning your day 24 hours in advance. When you sit down to start your day, you should already have your priorities and tasks mapped out for that day. Taking on this habit will make you more efficient while enabling you to serve your customers at a higher level because you are prepared.

ACTIVELY BUILD YOUR PIPELINE

This should go without saying because you cannot close sales without a full pipeline. However, one of the biggest mistakes sales professionals make is they stop feeding their pipeline once it gets full and starts to produce results. This is the last thing you want to do. You should always be feeding your pipeline. There is never a time when you should step back and rest your laurels. When you are building your pipeline in the beginning, yes, you will work harder because you are building it from scratch. Once your pipeline is full, you should continue to grow and add to it, maybe not at the level you were growing it from the beginning, but the goal should always be to keep it full. When you are just getting started, you will spend a lot of your time building your pipeline, but once you become more established, you will spend more time setting appointments and meeting with prospects; but you still need to make time for prospecting and adding to your pipeline, even if it's just 10-15% of your day. If you invest your time in doing this, your business will continue to grow.

NURTURE YOUR EXISTING CUSTOMERS

New sales professionals are so focused on getting new business, they often fall down on this part of the job, but it is essential. Who wants to do all of the work to win a customer just to lose them? That is exactly what will happen if you don't take the time to nurture your existing customers and show appreciation for them. Sales is not a set it and forget it business. Your customers need to know that you care about them. Don't play into the negative stereotype of the salesperson that is only concerned about getting the sale and doesn't care about the customer afterward. A customer that knows you care about them and are attentive to their needs will not only be loyal to you and your company, but they will also refer more business to you which is invaluable. When you are doing your daily planning, make sure you include simple touches to check in on your customers and show them some love.

BE A STUDENT OF YOUR BUSINESS

No matter what industry you're working in, things are constantly changing and evolving. Stand above your competition and let your customers and prospects know that you are serious about your business by being a student of your business. This means being aware of what the competition is doing and what is trending in the marketplace. You might need to pick up a book or two to stay on top of trends in the business. Also, pick a few blogs or news wires to follow to stay up to date on news in your industry. Your customers will appreciate your dedication to educating yourself on their business. It will also qualify you to be an advisor to better serve their needs.

SCHEDULE APPOINTMENTS DAILY

I'm sure you've heard that sales is a numbers game. We talked earlier about the importance of building your pipeline. An active pipeline will yield a certain number of appointments on your calendar per day. A great sales professional keeps a full calendar as a result of maintaining these habits we've just discussed.

I understand that change doesn't happen overnight. Learning and implementing these new habits will take some time, especially if you need to shed some of the old habits that we discussed earlier. Give yourself some grace as you work through the process and realize that it takes at least 21 days to establish a new habit. Track your progress with your new habits by keeping a notebook and acknowledging each time you complete one of these tasks. Keep doing this until it becomes muscle memory for you, and you begin to see the results from engaging in them.

DO YOU HAVE GOALS?

Now that you have begun to establish daily habits to feed your sales, those habits should funnel into a larger plan. That plan would be your goals. If you are seeking to accomplish anything in your life, you need to have goals. Otherwise, you are working toward nothing. The same is true of your sales goals. A salesperson without goals is just treading water.

Have you ever heard of the SMART formula when setting goals?

Specific
When setting your goals, you need to be specific in what you want to achieve. You don't want to set a broad goal that you want to achieve more sales this year than you did last year. Who doesn't? Be more specific in your approach. You can set a goal that you want to increase your sales by 10% over last year. Or, if your sales last year were $1.5 million, you could set a goal to increase it to $2 million this year, retaining your existing business. This is a specific goal.

Measurable
It is important that you are able to track your progress, so your goals do need to be measurable. Once you set your sales goal, you should be able to break it down into bite sized pieces of what you need to accomplish daily, weekly, monthly to achieve the goal. How do you eat an elephant? One bite at a time. Measuring your goal also allows you to make course corrections along the way, whether you are tracking above your goal and think you have room for increase, or if you're tracking below it and need to adjust down.

Achievable
Most sales professionals are ambitious so it is not uncommon for you to bite off more than you can chew when setting your initial goals. Be conservative when you set your goals, enabling you to blow your own mind when you exceed them. Setting an achievable goal that isn't too easy

but offers a challenge is a balancing act. A simple rule of thumb is to shoot for an increase, even if it is conservative. Study how you have been growing your sales over the past years and use that information to set a realistic and achievable goal for yourself.

Realistic
This overlaps the last point we just made as you want to make sure you set a realistic goal for yourself. Challenge yourself but if the goal you set is something you nor anyone in your department has ever done before, it's likely not a realistic goal. Take the pressure off of yourself and stick with numbers you feel comfortable with.

Timely
To achieve any goal, you will need a deadline. A deadline will build a sense of urgency for you to achieve the goal because you know that every day counts in moving forward to reach that goal.

PRACTICE

One of my favorite ways to relate to others is through sports analogies. In particular, one of my favorite sports is golf. As one who enjoys a good golf game during my leisure, I learned that there are quite a few parallels between the game of golf and sales.

Like all sports, you can never become good without practice. I've found that when I get on the course without much practice, I'm quite rusty in the first few strokes and it takes a while for me to regain my rhythm. The best of the best in the golf game such as Tiger Woods, Arnold Palmer and Jason Day, all have one thing in common. They practice every day. They hone their craft because they understand that natural talent alone will not win championships; it has to be nurtured. The same is true with sales. So, what if you have the natural gift of gab or you know how to build relationships with people. Without regular practice to constantly get better at what you do, you'll never be more than average, and I know that's not your goal or you wouldn't be reading this book. It doesn't matter how good you get at what you do, you never arrive. If Tiger Woods still has to practice before getting on the golf course, you certainly need to practice before picking up the phone or going into a sale meeting. Never take for granted the value of practicing one more time before the big game.

Adjust your game

A good golf professional knows when to adjust their game. If something is not working, they need to course correct. It is much easier to discover the areas that you need to adjust in practice rather than in a live game, which is why practice is so vital. Here's a fun fact: when a rocket flies to the moon, it has to course correct every couple of seconds to reach its destination. If a rocket flying to the moon has to course correct, why wouldn't you? Recognize when something is not working or if it is not yielding your anticipated results and be prepared to make a change, as needed.

Listen to Your Caddy

In golf, your caddy is your guide. From the outside looking in, many think a caddy's role is simply to carry the golfer's clubs, but it is so much more than that. Experienced caddies know the terrain of the golf course and the challenges that will be presented to the golfer during their game. The caddy works as a coach to the golfer to keep them on course. The best golfers listen to their caddies. As a sales professional, your caddy may be your mentor or sales manager. They are tasked with keeping you on course. They have more experience than you and know the terrain that you are navigating. Listen to your coach to avoid pitfalls and move toward your goals.

Whether your vice is golf or another sport, use it to help you gain clarity on your role as a sales professional and how you can elevate yourself to a higher level in achieving your set goals.

To this point, you've discovered your passion, you've begun to develop healthy habits that will lead to sales success, and you've developed SMART goals to guide your daily progress. In the next chapter, I'd like to share one of my proprietary approaches to sales that will help you stand above the rest.

B.U.D. STRATEGY FOR MINDSET

BETTER: Don't let yourself off the hook. Be accountable and set realistic goals.

UNIQUE: Always be prepared. Study your business which includes your client and take proactive steps to move the needle forward. Too often sales professionals work in a reactive nature. You instantly stand out the minute you choose to be proactive.

DESIRABLE: Golfers don't employ caddies that they don't desire to work with. They add value to them and help improve their game. Be the caddy for your prospect and your customer.

CASE STUDY: MINDSET

BROUN

Broun's story is a key example of how adopting the correct mindset can amplify and create opportunities in sales. Broun sought my guidance as a young professional just graduating from college and diving into the world of sales for the first time.

As a newbie to sales, Broun was interested in learning the step-by-step process to execute a strong sales strategy in his young career. Once I gave him a formula to follow with his sales, Broun began to see an increase in his output, productivity, and results.

After his first year working with me, Broun was able to have his first six figure year, selling over $100,000 which was a significant increase over his previous year. He accredits much of his success to developing the correct mindset and learning how to correctly manage his time and resources.

Broun learned how to schedule and organize his time to meet with his prospects and clients. He also learned the value of reviewing proposals with the client either in person or over the phone instead of just emailing them. Broun noted that scheduling times to follow up has been very important in his process.

Broun also implemented the politely persistent component of the B.U.D. process which we will discuss in the next chapter. In doing so, he emphasized the importance of always showing the prospect or client that you value their time.

Adopting a strong mindset and putting these strategies in place has enabled Broun to meet his sales goals on a consistent basis.

CHAPTER 4: PROSPECTING

When I say the word, prospecting, what are the first words that come to mind? Do those words emote a negative or positive emotion within you? For the most part, sales professionals are intimidated by the entire process of prospecting. It's the grunt work of sales. It's digging in the trenches and doing what is necessary, not what is fun. Most people equate prospecting directly with cold calling, and let's face it, if you love cold calling, you are, indeed, a rare breed. The truth is, there is more to prospecting than cold calling, and if sales professionals took the time to dissect the prospecting process, you might find yourself closing more sales. Until the sale is closed, and your prospect has been converted into a customer, you are prospecting. That means prospecting covers a lot of ground from the grunt work of cold calling and building your leads to cultivating those leads into prospects and turning them into customers. Are you ready to dive in?

ARE YOU CURIOUS?

I'm sure you're familiar with the term, 'curiosity killed the cat.' Lucky for you, you're not a cat. Curiosity is the framework for building a great relationship with your prospect and uncovering the root of their problems. Your prospects need to know that they are more than a number or dollar sign to you. The way you prove that to them is by asking questions to learn more about their business and how you can best serve them. This starts with being curious. If this process is new to you, you may need to begin by writing some questions down to ask your prospect, but eventually, you want this to become an organic process.

Listen actively to what they are saying and be prepared to ask more probing questions to dig deeper into the conversation. What will this accomplish for you in the sales process?

It will build trust. When your prospect sees that you genuinely care about their business and what they are trying to accomplish, they will let their guard down. Never assume that your prospect trusts you from the beginning, just because you appear to have a friendly relationship with them. Most prospects will have their guard up when it comes to sales professionals because too many have already come through their door with their own agenda and no regard for their needs. Prove them otherwise and show them how you're different by putting all of your attention on them.

It prepares you. In an earlier chapter, we discussed the importance of preparation during the sales process. The more you know, the better you are able to serve your prospect. It's possible you may have walked into the door thinking they needed one solution but after asking questions and learning more about them, you learn that they need something completely different. Never make assumptions. Asking questions and being curious allows you to solve your prospect's problems and give them exactly what they need.

Asking questions engages your prospect. When you meet with your prospect, it's not about you. It's about them. But the meeting should be a conversation. It shouldn't be completely one-sided. When you are asking questions and engaging, you are showing the prospect, not only that you care and want to learn more about their business, but also that you are listening. Be natural and listen to your instincts when you're talking to your prospect. Relax. This is a conversation. When they share information with you, ask follow-up questions to learn more. Always seek to learn more.

You learn about their business. There is value in learning about your prospect's business. If your prospect opens up and is willing to talk about the challenges in their business, let them. Knowledge is power. Perhaps you have other customers or prospects in the same industry with similar challenges. This will shed some light on how to address those issues.

It gets your prospect talking. In a sales appointment, you'd always rather have your prospect doing the talking rather than yourself. For one, it is a sign that they are feeling comfortable and relaxed with you. And two, as we just mentioned, it is an opportunity for you to learn more from what they are sharing. As the sales professional, it is imperative that you steer the conversation during an appointment, but always keep the prospect talking. That means you continue to ask good questions.

Asking good questions and being curious is something that will guide you throughout the sales process, from your first contact whether it's on the phone or online, through to your appointment. But let's talk a little bit about proper habits to develop during the prospecting process because one of our primary goals is to get the appointment with the prospect, but how do we get to that point?

Yes, prospecting does include the dreaded cold call, which we will discuss, but you will also learn that prospecting includes much more than making cold calls. As a matter of fact, the more you can diversify your outreach, the more effective you will be as a sales professional.

The first thing you must do when it comes to prospecting, is make a commitment to do it. I know it seems silly to say that, but you'd be surprised how many sales professionals lack results or their well runs dry because they don't take time to prospect. Some dread the task so they simply don't do it. Others may have started the process of building a good pipeline and as soon as they start to get results, they stop building. Well, guess what happens when you stop building your pipeline? You eventually run out of leads. You don't want this to be you, so it's imperative that you take time out of every day to focus on prospecting. Notice, I didn't say your whole day or that you need to take one or two days out of your week to focus on prospecting. I said every day, and I'm not even suggesting that much time – just one hour. One hour a day consistently will help you build and manage your sales pipeline. Even if you hate prospecting, I think you can manage one hour out of each day to devote to it. However, I'm hoping that after you finish reading this book, even those that hate prospecting, will gain a new respect for it, and at least learn to tolerate it, because it is a necessary cog in the wheel of your sales success.

For the purpose of this section on prospecting, we are going to focus on making cold or even warm calls. When you set aside the time each day to focus on your prospecting, it is important that you eliminate any distractions during this time. That means that you will want to plan your prospecting time around a time when you least expect to get customer calls and when you don't have appointments on the calendar. When you schedule appointments, schedule it around your prospecting hour. Yes, it is that important.

To maximize the use of your time, when you are prospecting, keep your objective singular. You are only trying to secure an appointment at this time. You don't need to go into a deep dive with the prospect, even if they seem receptive. Let them know that you are looking forward to meeting them and talking more about their business and their needs during your appointment. Your prospecting time is all about productivity and results. How many appointments can you create in an hour? You could even create a little contest with yourself to make it fun. Do whatever you feel you need to do to motivate you to pick up the phone and make that next call. While this is time meant to be productive and you are looking to produce numbers, I'm not suggesting that you rush a prospect off the call. Just be judicious about your time. When you build a rapport with someone, it is easy to get caught up in a conversation for fifteen minutes talking about golf swings. Save that for the appointment. Take the time to set your prospect at ease in the beginning of the conversation, but remember, your only objective in the beginning is to get the appointment.

Be prepared with your list prior to making calls. The last thing you want to do is waste your hour each day, searching for prospects to call. Your list should already be prepared, and you should have the name and/or number of the decision maker you need to speak with. There are many sources you can use to find the right person to speak with such as LinkedIn, Google, etc. We will discuss how to use the internet and social media as a resource a little later in this chapter.

When you schedule your prospecting, it is better to do it during off-peak hours. That means you should aim for early in the morning or late in the day. This allows you plenty of time to run your appointments and get everything you need to get done in the peak of your day. You may find during this process that you're not much of a morning person but many of your prospects are up early and in their office at 7 am. If that's the case, brew your coffee and get ready to make some early morning calls.

Where it is possible, try to vary your call times. If you find that you are calling a prospect at 10 am every day but not reaching them, this may not be an ideal time to call. Try 8:00 am the next time and keep varying until you see results. You are only blocking a small amount of time each day to work on your prospecting, so make it count.

Be organized. Keep accurate and detailed records of the prospects that you are reaching out to. This is where working with a customer relationship management (CRM) tool is very handy because it will allow you to set up call back times and manage your schedule more efficiently. If you don't have the luxury of a CRM system in your current role, try to use something like Google docs or your email system to keep track of notes and call back times.

In sales, it is always important to believe in what you do and have a plan for success. Prospecting is the very beginning of the sales process. Success at this stage is setting the appointment and then you take small steps toward the goal of closing at each stage. It is important that you understand what you are trying to accomplish when you sit down at your desk and make the first phone call. Your goal is not to try to close the sale on the first call. You simply want to book the appointment so that you can learn more about the prospect and propose the best solution. When you keep it simple, the process becomes easier to follow.

MANAGE THE PROCESS WITH YOUR PROSPECTS

You must manage the sales process with your prospects to keep them moving along the cycle. Remember, they are looking to you as the expert to guide them along. There are no magic steps to follow to manage your sales process. It's more of an intuitive act and will become much easier to manage as you gain more experience as a sales professional. You will learn that every prospect goes through the sales process differently based on their needs and their unique situation, and you need to respond in kind. There is no cookie cutter method to managing the process but there are some points I'd like to review that can guide you in the right direction, particularly if you are new to the process.

Earlier we talked about the importance of staying organized throughout the process. As part of that organization, make sure you are documenting every interaction you have with the prospect. This will help you stay organized and know what needs to be done at each stage with your customer. Remember, you are guiding them through the process which means, when done correctly, should be done seamlessly without the customer knowing. Set expectations with your customer during every interaction and make an effort to move the needle forward to get to the finish line.

There is never such a thing as a one-size-fits-all solution for any prospect. Take the time to understand their needs and learn their business. This is part of establishing trust and building a relationship with your prospect. Even if you offer a singular product, never assume that every customer will utilize that product in exactly the same way. Learn their story and work with them to fill the gaps in their process that need to be addressed. Be curious. We talked about this already. Your prospect already expects you to come into an appointment with your own agenda. Don't play into the salesperson stereotype. Show them that you have their best interest at heart and keep the conversation steered toward them.

After they've taken the time to share their needs and their business background with you, work with them to develop a collaborative solution to fit their needs. Why collaborative? Not only does this further engage the prospect but it educates them on the active role they need to play to put a proper solution in place. Part of that might be some changes they need to make in their habits to make room for your product. The obvious role they will need to play is fiscally making sure that their budget will allow them to move forward in the process with you. You are guiding the sales process on your end, but you are helping them guide the progression internally, to make sure all of the i's are dotted and t's are crossed to close the sale.

We've talked about techniques to manage your time when prospecting but what are some of the activities that you need to do as a sales professional to keep your pipeline full? How will you occupy that one hour a day that you set aside for prospecting? The obvious answer is by making phone calls but do all of those phone calls need to be cold? Not necessarily. Ultimately, you will need to determine what mix works best for you to create leads for your pipeline, but in the next chapter I will talk about a few strategies that have worked for me in building my sales career.

B.U.D. STRATEGY FOR PROSPECTING

BETTER: *Don't let yourself off the hook. Be accountable and set realistic goals.*

UNIQUE: *Always be prepared. Study your business which includes your client and take proactive steps to move the needle forward. Too often sales professionals work in a reactive nature. You instantly stand out the minute you choose to be proactive.*

DESIRABLE: *Golfers don't employ caddies that they don't desire to work with. They add value to them and help improve their game. Be the caddy for your prospect and your customer.*

CHAPTER 5: NETWORKING

Networking can be a fantastic tool to grow your sales pipeline if you know how to utilize it correctly. One of the greatest time savers that evolved from our 2020 pandemic crisis was more virtual meetings. While meeting in person is still valuable, virtual meetings allow you to save time on the road and still connect with people online. If there are opportunities for you to try out or connect with networking groups virtually, it's a great way to save time and be more efficient.

Some people hate the idea of networking and if you go into a meeting without a goal or objective, I can see how the process can be grueling. It's also important to choose the right group that will meet your needs and put you in front of the right people. But first, you must understand that networking isn't about trying to make a sale on the spot. It is first about building relationships. You will find that when you network correctly, some of the relationships that will evolve from the process will become your customers, while others will become valuable referral partners. Both can help you build and grow your sales pipeline. Networking is not a selfish act. It's about give and take. Are you familiar with Zig Ziglar's quote, "if you help enough people get what they want, you will get what you want?" That is the very essence of networking.

So how do you make the most of networking and use it as a tool to fuel your pipeline?

Like everything else we've talked about so far, you must be prepared. Never walk into the room without an objective. Know what it is that you want to accomplish. That doesn't mean that you go in with the intention to sell, but you do need to know what you're looking for. Who is your ideal prospect? Is there someone in particular that you are looking to meet or get introduced to? Understand what you want to accomplish before you get there. Also, come prepared with plenty of business cards. You want to make it easy for people to contact you after you make a connection. Like I mentioned earlier, don't go in with selfish ambitions. Be prepared to help others and make connections for them as well. The more generous you are in helping others, the more rewards you will receive in return.

I cannot stress the importance of finding the right group. There are so many networking groups out there these days, you could make a career out of just attending meetings. That is not what you want to do. Instead, you want to try out a few groups to see if they have the people you are trying to connect with. If you go to a group and it's not a good fit, it's okay. Move on to the next one. Don't allow yourself to become overwhelmed by thinking you need to go to every group that you're invited to. Determine the best criteria for your networking groups and filter each group through that. Once you've determined a few groups that work for you, keep it to just a few. Again, you don't want to make a career of going to meetings or you'll never have time to sell. I'd suggest starting with 2-3 groups maximum and if you have other groups that you'd like to join in the future, maybe you just switch it up a little. Take the time to commit to the groups that you are in, because you will have a responsibility to give and help them grow their business just as you expect them to help you grow your own.

Once you select a few groups to belong to, make sure you're an active member of that group. If you want to get value and results out of your groups, you must be intentional to build relationships and contribute. Don't expect to just show up every week and get results. You will have to work for it.

One of your primary reasons to join a networking group is to receive referrals and to feed your sales pipeline. But remember, in networking, like any relationship, there is a give and take. It is important that you actively work to give referrals to the people in your group if you expect to receive them. This is part of being an active participant in your groups.

Networking is a very effective way to grow your business but there is no timeline on how you do this. Be patient and trust the process. Do the work and the results will come. Just because you don't close a sale within your first week or you haven't received any hot leads doesn't mean that networking is not working for you.

Enjoy the process. Networking doesn't need to be grueling. It can and should be something that you look forward to.

USING SOCIAL MEDIA TO NETWORK

LinkedIn and other professional social media platforms are excellent tools to prospect for new business, but they do require a degree of finesse to utilize it correctly. One of the biggest mistakes I see sales professionals make when attempting to use social media to grow their pipeline is being too salesy. No one really wants to be sold to, especially on social media. Instead, you must attempt to build a relationship with them. Consider the tips we went over for networking. A lot of the same applies when you are social networking, except you are privy to a lot more information on the person you are seeking to connect with.

Be strategic in your approach. You don't have to start off cold. Look at the people who have already engaged with you and start there. These are warm leads. Ask yourself if they fit the profile of your ideal customer. If so, make an attempt to connect with them via a private message, but don't start off with a sales pitch. If it's been some time since you've last connected, find a common ground to re-establish your connection with them. Look at the posts they have commented on or a post they recently created and comment on it. Be authentic. Use this connection to build and expand your relationship with this individual.

Make sure you have an updated profile. As you begin to engage more people on social media, they will check out your profile to learn more about you. What do you want them to see? What kind of impression do you seek to make? In LinkedIn, for example, often your first impression is your profile, so it is worth it to take the time to optimize it and provide detailed information on who you are and what you do. Make sure to include an up to date, professional photo of yourself because a picture does speak a thousand words.

Your connections are going to be more likely to engage with you when they see that you are active on social media. Make an effort to publish and post on the platform at least daily. Provide information of value, as this starts to establish you as an expert in what you do. The more you do this, the more you will begin to attract people to you that are interested in what you do and what you have to say. As you begin to attract more people to you, you will also be able to analyze more data regarding their demographics and whether or not they fit your ideal customer profile.

Tap into the power of groups. Getting involved with groups enables you to engage on a deeper level. It also allows you to be more targeted in the people you are networking with, making your efforts more efficient.

Be personal and authentic when connecting with people. I cannot stress this enough. People can see through fake intentions and often know when you are just trying to connect with them to achieve an agenda. Remember, as a sales professional, you are a problem solver. Your goal is to build meaningful connections and when you see an opportunity to fill a gap or solve a problem, offer a solution. It's as simple as that.

One of the strengths of LinkedIn is the ability to view who has viewed your profile. This provides great insight for you as a sales professional and opens the door for you to communicate with them. They are curious, at best, to learn more about you if they are exploring your profile. Take the time to introduce yourself to them if you haven't already done so. If you have in the past, take the time to re-connect.

When engaging on social media, take your time. Don't be overly anxious or expect to see results right away. Remember, you are building relationships and that takes time. One of the flaws of many sales professionals is the need to move quickly. I understand that you want to make sales or that you might have a quota to meet but you can't rush the process. That is the reason why it's important to have a good marketing mix to prospect so that you don't put too much pressure on any one activity to yield results. If you are just beginning the process of building your online presence, it will take time to build those relationships authentically and connect with the people you seek. However, once you take the time to build that engine, it will yield results for you that are one hundred-fold.

If you or your company is willing to invest in some of the more in-depth tools within LinkedIn, for example, you might want to try out the sales navigator. The sales navigator was designed with you in mind. The sales navigator not only allows you to actively search for opportunities that match your needs, but it also syncs with your CRM system, enabling you to track your activity and communication with these leads. One of the best features of the sales navigator is its intuitive ability to recommend leads for you. Based on the leads you've looked up and saved, the sales navigator will make recommendations of similar leads for you to pursue. The TeamLink filter allows you to conduct a search of possible leads that share connections with you, whether it is on a first, second or third level. This is a perfect opportunity for you to engage someone in your network and possibly ask for an introduction.

If you're comfortable with social media, I'd recommend that you utilize the video feature to connect a little bit more with your audience. Video is one of the top-rated media strategies used to connect with your audience. Therefore, if you use video in any of your media, you're likely to receive more engagement. Your video doesn't have to be long. Start out with something about 1-2 minutes and maybe offer a simple tip that might be helpful to your target audience. Get into the habit of sharing in this capacity on a consistent basis and observe how your audience reacts.

Consider creating shareable content. This is beyond the daily posts that we discussed earlier. If you don't already have a blog, consider starting one. The purpose of this content would be to connect and educate your audience on your industry and what you do. Share that content online. Doing so will solidify your position with your audience as an expert and create more opportunities to engage. Another way to create shareable content is to write articles or posts. Consider writing one to two articles a week to share with your connections. Like everything else, give it time. Don't give up too soon if you don't see a ton of engagement with your first few articles. A lot of people like to sit back and watch you first before they attempt to engage. That does not mean they are not reading your articles or that they are not paying attention. Stay consistent and you will begin to see results over time.

One of the biggest complaints for many people when it comes to any form of social media is the time commitment. Yes, it does take time because you are building a relationship. You do need to schedule time into your calendar on a regular basis to engage with your audience if you are serious about using social media as a platform to build and grow your leads. But there are also tools that you can use to save time as well. Scheduling tools such as Hootsuite and Buffer will allow you to schedule your posts in advance to save you some time. I would suggest that you plan your content out in advance, load into the scheduling tool, and then plan a certain amount of time each week to engage on the platform. The combination of these actions will yield the positive results that you seek. Don't get complacent with the scheduling tools and just think you can set it and forget it. Social media doesn't work that way. You have to engage.

When you're looking for a way to connect with someone authentically, take the time to study their profile in advance of contacting them. What are their likes and dislikes? What kind of content do they follow? This will provide some insight into the type of conversation you can have with them. Use the information in their profile along with their posts to decipher your initial conversation with them.

I could write another book on how to utilize social media to build your sales pipeline, but these are just a few tips to get you started. One of the most important things to consider when prospecting is to diversify your mix. There are going to be some activities that you do that yield more results than others. Tilt the scales to favor those activities but never put all of your eggs in one basket. Be creative in seeking new ways to connect with and engage with your prospects.

B.U.D. STRATEGY FOR NETWORKING

BETTER: If you're not using social media to network, you're missing out in a big way. Make sure you have a professional and complete profile and that you're actively engaging with people, groups, and content.

UNIQUE: Leveraging a professional social media platform is one of the ways your prospects can get to know you before they even start doing business with you. Share posts from professionals in the industry you respect and write content about how you do business. Then, when someone is looking for your product/service, they will think of you.

DESIRABLE: Connecting with other experts and professionals will increase your credibility. And, if you're well connected, others will look to you for recommendations and referrals. Think of it this way: you would ask a friend, family member, or colleague for a referral to find the right product or service, why not replicate this same interaction online, if possible? Then everyone wins.

CASE STUDY: PROSPECTING

CRYSTAL

When I first started working with Crystal, she'd just started her project management business. Sales was unfamiliar to her. She didn't even know where to begin. She began working with me through an introductory course where she learned the basic fundamentals of sales, such as how to grow her business and identify her target market. She also learned how to improve her online presence.

Over a year later, Crystal re-engaged with me after gaining more clarity on her business and taking time to practice the strategies she'd learned. I worked with her to formulate her sales strategy. She learned the basics of her sales cycle and how to follow up and we took a deeper dive into LinkedIn. Crystal learned the value of follow up and staying in touch with people. I gave her specific ideas to implement touch points with her prospects and clients and she was a sponge, listening to everything I taught her. Following my coaching, Crystal was able to land her first $30,000 client after working with me for a short time.

Being able to land that contract and go on to land more clients like that, Crystal attributes learning her sales cycle to being able to effectively grow her business. She never understood the value of the sales cycle and its importance before going over it with me.

Crystal went on to have her best year in business after our coaching, yielding a 20% increase after implementing the strategies I taught. She said her weekly conversations held her accountable to create results. More than anything, she didn't want to let me down.

JOHN

John was another sales manager that I worked with, but he was more interested in implementing social selling with his team. Understanding the value of social media and how it can impact sales today, he sought my coaching to teach him and his team how to leverage social media for prospecting and sales opportunities.

John wanted to increase the social selling footprint for the company, and he knew that he needed some guidance to accomplish this goal. I worked with John and his team to teach best practices for social media, some of which were outlined in this chapter. I taught him how to use the right process in utilizing this social media platform and how to be strategic. This is a very important element when developing your presence, because like so many social media platforms, it is easy to scroll and waste time. You can like as many posts as you want and make as many comments as you want but if you don't have a strategy in place, you are just wasting time. In developing your strategy, I taught John to ask himself, what problem is he trying to solve, and then run all his actions through that funnel.

John set search engines to drive more opportunities and worked with his team to focus on these opportunities. After our coaching, John was able to accomplish his goal of expanding their social footprint. Their social footprint grew by over 15% after our work together. John was happy to report that their team has made social media a part of their sales process and they continue to use online tools to their advantage and continue to expand their social footprint.

CHAPTER 6: THE APPOINTMENT

Your primary goal during the prospecting process is to get the appointment. Once the prospect says yes for the first time, what happens next? How do you prepare for the first appointment with your potential customer?

Earlier, we talked about the importance of preparation. This is what separates the good from the great in the world of sales. Before you have your first appointment with your prospect, you want to prepare.

SET PROPER EXPECTATIONS

When you speak with the prospect on the phone and they agree to meet with you, set the proper expectations of what your meeting will entail. If there is anything that the prospect should bring to the meeting to make it more effective, let them know when you book the appointment. There is nothing wrong with asking the prospect to fully participate in this process. The more engaged they are, the better your results. You also want to make sure you make the best use of their time and yours.

SET A GOAL FOR YOUR MEETING

Know exactly what you want to accomplish in the meeting, even if it is to book another meeting. The sales process is going to vary based on the company and product you are selling so that will often impact how many meetings it will take to close the sale. Your goal may be to prepare a quote for the prospect at the end of the meeting. Just make sure that you go into the meeting with a clear objective. Otherwise, you might find yourself wasting time or walking out of a meeting without moving the needle forward.

DO YOUR HOMEWORK

This is where preparation comes in, and where you can rise above the competition. If it feels like you are doing too much work, chances are, you need to be doing it. When you have your initial conversation with the prospect, you should be asking probing questions to learn what their pain points are, but your detective work does not stop there. Take the time to research more about their company and these pain points so that you walk into the appointment armed with the best solutions designed to meet their specific needs.

PROVIDE A SOLUTION

A trap that many sales professionals fall into when they go into an appointment, is they start the appointment offering their solutions. How can you provide solutions if you have not uncovered their pain point? Yes, I understand that you've discussed this during your phone call and then you did your homework. When you arrive at the appointment, you want to expand on that knowledge. The prospect will, no doubt, provide you with more information to help you provide the best solution to their needs. Direct the questions and let them talk. You will uncover more information about their needs in the appointment than you did over the phone because you will have begun to set the prospect at ease. The more they trust you, the more they will share. The more information they share, the more you are leveraged to provide the best solutions to attack their problem. When they tell you their problems, LISTEN. I cannot stress this enough. It is impossible for you to provide the best solution if you don't listen to what they are telling you. After you've given the prospect the time to go over their pain points, now you can develop a solution. It's possible that you might need to go back to the drawing board to sketch out a solution for them, and that's okay. You don't have all of the answers in the first appointment.

NEXT STEPS

Never leave an appointment without a clear objective of the next step in the process. For example, if you spent the first appointment focused on the prospect and their pain points (which isn't a bad idea, by the way), set a second appointment with them to go over the best solutions to address their pain points. At each stage of the sales process, book a time with your prospect to move them to the next stage. It's possible that each stage is another meeting, or it could be a video call. Just make sure to put something on their calendar to keep them engaged and moving through the process with you.

Let's talk a little bit about the importance of booking that next meeting. As a sales professional, you must be intentional to ensure that you are able to get back in front of that prospect. One of the first ways to do this is to summarize what was covered in the first meeting and set the expectation with the prospect of what is coming next. Let them know that you want to be respectful of their time. For example, if you booked a thirty-minute appointment with them, stick to that thirty-minute window out of respect for their calendar. At the conclusion of your meeting, let them know what the next steps in the process are and book another time on their calendar. Just the fact that you were true to your word in respecting their time and sticking to your thirty minutes will likely increase your chances of getting that second meeting booked.

Be appreciative of the time they've taken to meet with you. While you are trying to provide a product or service that will make their life and business easier, you want to thank them for taking the time out of their schedule to meet with you.

One of the biggest mistakes that sales professionals make at the conclusion of a meeting is taking the queue from the prospect when they say something like, 'let's talk in a couple of weeks.' This can sometimes allow your prospect to go into the black hole where you are chasing them to get their time. Avoid this by simply booking a time with them during this meeting to discuss the next steps. Even if that happens to be in a couple of weeks, book that time on the calendar with a specific agenda to follow and an action plan to move the process forward.

B.U.D. STRATEGY FOR THE APPOINTMENT

BETTER: Be prepared and set goals for your appointment. Don't go in there rogue. Know exactly what you're trying to accomplish and you're likely to accomplish it.

UNIQUE: Salespeople are known for being talkers. It's what gives them a bad reputation in the marketplace. Stand out from the crowd by giving your prospect the floor. The more they talk, the more you learn. Listen.

DESIRABLE: Show respect for the time that the prospect has given you. If you only asked for thirty minutes of their time, don't take an hour. Thank them for the time they've given you and schedule a time to follow up to continue moving the process forward.

CASE STUDY: THE APPOINTMENT

JOE

Joe has been running an entrepreneurship training program for veterans for 10 years. One of the challenges that he has encountered with his program participants is anxiety and fear over engaging in sales. I connected with Joe on LinkedIn, and he shared his dilemma and wanted to develop a way to get his program participants more comfortable with the sales process.

I worked with Joe to create workshops and seminars for his participants around the sales process from setting the appointment to closing. Through these workshops, I worked with these participants to teach them the true definition of sales and what was involved in every stage of the process. I also taught them how to use LinkedIn as a tool to connect with their prospects.

One of the biggest takeaways from these training sessions was helping them to understand the true nature of the first appointment. You are not trying to close the sale on the first appointment; you simply want to book the next appointment.

I continue to host workshops for Joe and his team to help them understand how to use sales in their budding business ventures.

CHAPTER 7: BUILDING RAPPORT & RELATIONSHIPS

One of the primary ways to get your prospects to book an appointment with you is by building an emotional connection. We talked earlier about the importance of building trust, and you will learn that this happens throughout the sales process. However, at the very beginning of the process, it is important to steer everything toward them and their needs (which should be your intention anyway) to build trust and move them further along in the sales process.

One of the first ways to break the communication barrier between you and your prospect is to know and understand their business. It is not necessary that you do extensive research at the beginning of the process when you are trying to get the appointment, however, you should know enough about their business to show them that you have done your homework. This will demonstrate to them that they are not just another sales call for you. Instead of asking or interviewing them about their business, show them that you understand their business. They will be impressed that you took the time to learn more about them and be willing to open up more to you, and then, of course, schedule an appointment with you where you can dig deeper.

Doing your homework and learning about their business sets your prospect at ease and shows that you care. Many sales professionals fail to realize that there is an emotional connection to the sales process and failure to tap into this emotional connection will result in loss of sales and results. A big part of building your relationship with your prospect is building trust. The first building block of this foundation is doing your homework and learning about their business, which we've already identified.

Next, you want to leverage yourself as an expert. No one wants to be sold, but many professionals seek the advice of a coach or consultant. This is the role you are stepping into with your prospect. By showing extensive knowledge of your field and what you do, you continue to nurture and grow that trust with your prospect. To be knowledgeable in your field in addition to their business does require a great deal of preparation and a lot of time and education. However, if you want to elevate yourself to the best of the best in your field, these actions are necessary. Don't try to shortcut the process by only researching and educating yourself on surface information.

Be authentic. Frauds will always be revealed over time; don't let that be you. Show your prospect that you take your work and their business seriously. They will, in turn, take you seriously.

Part of your job is not only to uncover what the prospect wants by researching their business and asking probing questions, but to also clarify their wants to make sure it aligns with their needs. This is part of being a good consultant. By understanding their business, you can study and make note of what they want and as you learn more about their business structure and needs and uncover a more refined solution that they might not have even realized they needed from the beginning. Your prospect will thank you and appreciate your expertise in uncovering such needs, as it further demonstrates that you know what you're doing, solidifying their trust in you.

As you are asking questions to learn more about their process and what they are currently doing, find out about the competition. This may include their current solution and/or other solutions they may be considering. It is imperative that you do not bash the competition as this will taint your credibility and professionalism with the prospect. Instead, compliment the competition on what they are doing well. We will review more about how to handle your competition later in this book. Allow the prospect to reveal to you flaws they see in your competition. If their current solution isn't meeting their needs, find out why and what their challenges are. This is part of your research in helping them determine the best solution to meet their needs, whether it ends up being you or your competition.

While you are working with your prospect early in the process, learn what their timeline is. This is both for your benefit and theirs. For you, the last thing you want to do is put the prospect in your pipeline for the next three months if their timeline is eighteen months. The unfortunate result of such actions is usually undue pressure placed on the prospect to close within your timeline when they told you at the outset that this was a marathon approach. If there is a sense of urgency for your customer to deliver a solution immediately, make sure you set the correct expectations conversely. For example, if they need to have a solution in place within the next two weeks but your operations team cannot deliver a solution for four weeks, be candid with the customer to see if there is still a possibility to work together. They will appreciate your honesty well above disappointment.

We talked about asking probing questions at the outset of the appointment and during the appointment, but don't allow yourself to get lazy with asking questions as you move further throughout the sales process with your prospect. It's important that you remain curious and ask questions at every stage of the process. This avoids confusion and ensures you and the prospect stay on the same page.

Early in your first appointment, remember to set your expectations with the client. Help them to understand that you are seeking information and expect them to give information. It's important that they understand this relationship to be a give and take. Sales professionals have a bad reputation of being takers and a lot of prospects expect you to walk into the sales appointment and just launch into a presentation that is all about you. Don't perpetuate that stereotype. Be direct with your prospect in letting them know the purpose of the appointment and what you expect to accomplish as a result.

Small talk does set your client at ease but keep it at a minimum. As you learn the different characteristics of various personality types, you will learn that some prospects value more small talk than others. However, in the beginning, keep it short, maybe five minutes. You want to stay true to your promise when you booked the appointment. Whether your appointment is thirty minutes or an hour, organize your meeting to stay on track for that timeline. Remember that your prospect didn't book an appointment with you for small talk. They do want to talk business with you, so honor that.

There is a delicate balance to running your first appointment, and quite honestly, the best way to strike that balance correctly each and every time is with practice and repetition. Just as it is important not to dwell on small talk too long, you also don't want to launch into your solution too soon. We talked about ways to get your prospect to open up more to you about their business. I would suggest starting here. Learn what their pain points are and expand on some of the topics that you discussed with them when you booked the appointment. It's not likely that you'll be able to launch into a solution without gaining more information anyway. Take your time to make sure you are giving your prospect what they want and need.

When you get to the point in the process where you are offering a solution to the client, take a moment to put yourself in their shoes. Ask yourself, if you were them, would you buy from you? Are you authentic? Are you believable? Despite the common saying, this is not your 'dog and pony show.' Your prospect is looking to you to make a real connection. They want to know if you are just launching another sales presentation, or if you actually care about presenting them with a viable solution that will make their life and work better. You want to make sure you're answering the inevitable prospect question, "what's in it for me?" It's the reason why you focus on benefits rather than features when you are presenting a solution to your prospect. If you've done your homework as we've already discussed in earlier chapters, then you know the pain points of your prospect. Therefore, it is irrelevant to focus on products or services that don't speak to the direct needs of your prospect. There is no rule that says you must go through every aspect of your canned presentation, even if it doesn't pertain to your prospect or their direct needs. Don't be lazy when it comes to preparation and making sure you are responding directly to the needs of your prospect. Tell them what's in it for them. Let them know why they should be doing business with you. Tell them the direct benefits of implementing your product or service in their business. In other words, let them know how doing business with you is going to simplify their life and business by solving their problems. Prioritize what it is that they need to fix now. It is possible that they need multiple solutions and perhaps their budget only allows for them to address one or two at a time. Don't use that as an excuse not to close the sale. Find out what is needed most at the time and focus on that. You can always come back to the other solutions later.

When it comes to cost, make sure that you are building value with your prospect. Never get into the price game with your prospect or you'll never win. It's all about building value with them. What is your product or service worth to them? More importantly, how much money is being lost daily/weekly as a result of not having your product in place? Paint the picture for them to eliminate price objections. Help them to see the value of your product or service above and beyond their investment. Speaking of investment, help them to understand what this means. An investment means that they are receiving a return. Show them what that return looks like.

Understand the emotion that is connected with the buying process. Despite what many people may think, buying is emotional and you need to make room for that. Your prospect is going through an emotional roller coaster through the buying process, from feeling like they can't do without your product or service, to becoming afraid to make the move or investment. Give them grace through this process and work with them. This is why it is imperative to build a strong relationship with your prospect. Remember, people buy from people they like. In the end, they are not really buying the product, they are buying you. Build the know, like, trust factor and connect with your prospect emotionally and you will move the sales process to the next level.

EVALUATING COST

Let's revisit price for a moment because price is the number one objection that you will encounter and while we are not discussing objections just yet, you should be prepared to discuss price with your prospect. There are certainly going to be times when your prospect will tell you that your competition is coming in less than you. My first advice to you is not to freak out and act rashly. Don't bash the competition and talk about everything they can't do. Keep a level head and remember exactly what your prospect wants. Review their pain points with them again and the solution that you are providing. Conversely, review with them what your competition is offering for the lesser price. Emphasize again, value and how you can put money back in their pockets by working together. If you can beat your prospect to the punch by discussing price before they even bring it up, you put yourself in a position with more leverage to discuss this topic with your prospect. For example, there is nothing wrong with letting the prospect know early in the conversation that you're not the cheapest solution available (if you're not), because you're not selling price. Go on from there to share with them why you're the best solution for them and meeting their needs. It's also important to know that price should never be the end all be all when it comes to your solution. As I said earlier, no one ever truly wins when the decision is made solely on price. For example, you might win the business on price, but can you keep it? Keeping your customer long term and building a true relationship will not be based on how much they spent.

Rather, they are likely to continue working with you if you are able to meet their needs.

GET IN THE PROSPECT'S HEAD

As you are working through the appointment with your prospect, it's important to understand things from their perspective. I mentioned earlier that you need to put yourself in their shoes, so let's attempt to do that.

1. **The first question that your prospect is wondering about you is, "Are you dependable and reliable?"** Instead of waiting for the prospect to ask this question, why not address it yourself. Set your prospect at ease by showing them how dependable and reliable you are. You can do this by sharing some of your success in other projects or offering references to again, set your prospect at ease.

2. **The next question is, "do you do what you say you're going to do?"** This is a question of trust, and you will have to invest some time to gain the trust of your prospect. Part of this is just being authentic. There is no better way to answer this question for your prospect than to just demonstrate it.

3. **Question number three is, "do you do it when you say you're going to do it?"** This is an easy one because you can show this just in how you show up for the appointment. Respect their time. If you say you're going to schedule a 30-minute appointment, stick with it. Simple actions like this will build trust with your prospect that you will follow through in meeting all other deadlines that you set with them. Don't let them down.

4. ***Question four is, "do you do it right the first time?"***
   This is a tricky one because as a salesperson, you want
   to just say yes to satisfy the customer. But that is not
   always the right answer if it's not the truth. Your
   prospect is always going to respect a candid answer
   here. It is always better to answer truthfully and let your
   prospect know that there are times when you might not
   get it right the first time, but that you will work with them
   to perfect it until it is. They'd prefer this to you telling
   them yes and falling short.

5. ***Lastly, the prospect is wondering "do you get it
   done on time?"*** If the prospect has a timeline that they
   are anticipating getting their goal accomplished, you
   have a responsibility to be realistic on whether or not
   you can meet this need. Do not commit to something
   you know you will not be able to follow through on. This
   will cause more damage than good; just be honest. Let
   your prospect know whether or not you can meet their
   needs and expectations and work from there.

BE A CONSULTANT, NOT A SALESPERSON

Earlier, I mentioned that it is important that you leverage
yourself as an expert or consultant over a sales professional
because ultimately, no one wants to be sold.

Part of being a sales consultant is learning how to effectively
manage the sales process. This means knowing how to
sync your selling process with the customer's buying
process. This goes back to doing your homework and being
prepared. When you ask the right questions and understand
what your customer needs and what their process is, you
are able to synchronize this process seamlessly.

A good sales consultant has a good reputation among their customers and associates. Be prepared for your prospects to check up on you. They will ask around to learn more about you and your company. Build a solid reputation to leverage yourself as an expert in your field.

Being an expert in your field comes with responsibility. It's more than educating yourself through articles and videos. You should become familiar with your prospect and their needs on every level. Never stop learning and never stop asking questions.

A good consultant knows how to present well. It is expected by your prospect that you will be able to share information fluidly and be knowledgeable about subject matter.

After you've presented and moved forward to discuss solutions with your prospect, it is important to identify the budget of your prospect. This can sometimes be a little difficult to extract as prospects are often tight lipped about their budget as they attempt to play the game with you to get you to reveal your numbers first.

LEARN THE PHASES OF THE BUYING CYCLE

I mentioned earlier that you want to strike a delicate balance between the prospect's buying cycle and your own sales cycle. While each prospect will have a unique cycle when it comes to their timeline and process, there are some commonalities among the buying cycle that you want to always be cognizant of.

The first phase of the cycle is the status quo. This is where education becomes a big part of your role as a consultant and sales professional. In this case, your prospect has become comfortable and complacent in their current situation. You may observe there is no sense of urgency to make a move. It can be a very difficult part of the process because your prospect is not fully engaged, and in some cases, many sales professionals walk away, leaving a potential opportunity on the table. In some cases, you may not be able to sway the prospect; however, in most cases, simply educating them on their needs and the outcome of not taking action will spur engagement. Be diligent. This is one of the most difficult stages of the buying cycle and it occurs early, when you are still in the process of building the relationship and establishing trust with the client. Taking the time to invest in uncovering their needs will earn their respect and admiration, not to mention their business.

Phase two of the buying cycle is when your prospect actually recognizes their needs. This will come either through your education through the status quo or their discomfort in their current situation. Either way, the prospect has recognized they have a problem that needs to be addressed. As the sales professional, you must become the detective at this stage to uncover as much as possible to provide the best possible solution to your prospect. I mentioned the importance of asking good, probing questions and this is essential as you investigate and uncover the root problems of your prospect and how you can best offer a solution.

After you've played the role of detective, you must now present some options to your prospect. At stage three, your prospect has acknowledged their challenge and they are ready to make a change. They've moved out of the passive stage into active mode. At this stage, your prospect is meeting with you and your competitors to determine the best solution to meet their needs. Take your time during this stage to learn the true pain points of your prospect so that you can develop the best customized solution to meet their needs. Don't focus on what the competition is doing. If you do your homework properly and develop your solution in kind, you will likely stand out from the majority of your competition from the start.

The next stage in the buying process is called the resolution of concerns. At this stage, your prospect has identified a vendor that they want to partner with, but with questions. If you've made it to this stage in the buying process, it's not the end of the road. You have not closed the sale just yet, so don't get overconfident. The prospect clearly likes what you have to offer but they have not made a full commitment just yet. You still have to prove yourself. At this stage, you need to reiterate your value proposition and set your prospect at ease that you will be able to resolve their challenges. Go over exactly how you plan to do that along with your estimated timeline and the direct benefit to the prospect for doing so.

After the prospect has gone over their concerns, the next stage in the buying process is making a decision. At this point, you have convinced your prospect that you will be able to solve their problem with your solution and they are ready to sign on the dotted line.

The sixth stage of the buying process is implementation. This is where you get to prove that you do what you say you're going to do. Just because your prospect has signed on the dotted line and become your new customer doesn't mean that your job ends here. Your new customer is waiting to see if you are actually good for your word. They have trusted that you will be but that still remains to be seen. It's important that you nurture the relationship through this process and ensure your new customer has a good experience. Not only will a good experience lead to positive referrals that will continue to grow your book of business, but the opposite effect would result in a ruined reputation on your part that can affect future sales. The only thing that travels faster than good news is bad news. Don't become a victim of that because you abandoned the process too early.

The last part of the buying process is evaluating changes over time. Companies are always in a state of flux, so there will be changes that you need to monitor throughout the life cycle of your customer so that you can keep them informed. You shouldn't disappear from communication with your customer once you've closed them. Make a habit of keeping in consistent communication with them to maintain the relationship. This will allow you to stay ahead of changes such as changes in staff or ownership. You don't want your entire account to be compromised because you failed to stay in contact and a new point of contact has moved in that has no relationship with you. By staying engaged, you can stay ahead of changes like this and be ready to introduce yourself to the new contact upon arrival and work to build a relationship with them, renewing the company's confidence in you and your abilities.

If you make an effort to stay alert and engaged not only through your sales process, but also through the customer's buying process, you are sure to not only close the sale with your new customer but retain them as well.

Getting back to the appointment, to keep the sales process moving, it's important to book a meeting from a meeting. You don't want to leave any gap that might stall the sales process. Therefore, you want to keep your prospect engaged and ready to take the next step.

We've touched on this before but make sure that you are summarizing the current meeting and what you've accomplished so far. Outline the sales process with the prospect and set expectations. Give the prospect some homework to allow them to take ownership of the process so that they can take steps to prepare for the next meeting, and then, of course, set a date and time on the calendar.

Next, you want to make sure that the key decision makers are involved in the process. Don't be afraid to ask who is involved in the evaluation process of your products and services. Learn what their process looks like and how they make buying decisions. Involve those key players in your next meeting to move the process along.

Thank the prospect for taking the time to share their goals with you and carve time out of their schedule. Always let them know how much you respect their time.

B.U.D. STRATEGY FOR BUILDING RAPPORT & RELATIONSHIPS

BETTER: Build trust with your prospect by seeking to know and understand their business. This requires research before you talk to them. Be a detective.

UNIQUE: It's unfortunate but the term 'sales' has a bad reputation among most of your prospects. They expect you to take advantage of them for your own agenda. Flip this thinking by acting as a consultant rather than a salesperson. Your goal is to assess their problems and help them come up with a solution that will best serve them. Work alongside your prospect as a partner. Become an advisor to them.

DESIRABLE*: Get into your prospect's head and understand how they think. Be observant and respond to that thinking. It shows that you are intuitive and responsive to what they need.*

CHAPTER 8: DEALING WITH OBJECTIONS

One of the first rules of sales is if you are not encountering objections throughout the sales process, you are not doing it right. The prospect will naturally object to something in the process out of curiosity. If there are no objections, your prospect is not truly engaged, and you risk losing the sale. Let's discuss some of the primary objections you will deal with in the sales process and how to address them.

Price/budget. The number one sales objection that you will encounter in your process is price or budget. The prospect may say that your product is too expensive or that they lack the budget to afford it. If they say that your product is too expensive, counteract it by discussing value. Break down the numbers with your prospect and help them evaluate what it is costing them daily/weekly/monthly not to have your solution in place. Are they losing money by not having a solution in place? How much are they losing and how much would they be gaining by purchasing your product? Help them see a different perspective when it comes to price. After you go over these ratios with them, you can show them how you are saving them rather than costing them. Leverage your solution as an investment, not a cost or liability. When it comes to managing their budget, use the same reasoning. Help them understand how this investment will put dollars back in the company's pocket. If they have a definitive budget and can only spend a certain amount at the time, work with them to see if there are portions of your solution that you can prioritize now within their budget and implement the rest later. It is rare that your prospect will not bring up price as an objection. Always be prepared to handle this rebuttal in the sales process.

I don't need this right now. We just talked about this in the last chapter. It's the first stage of the buying cycle and a lot of prospects will put you through this to test your skills and make you work. Practice your expertise and put your detective hat back on. Investigate with your prospect what their true pain points are. Ask probing questions to uncover the nature of their problem. It is possible they have problems they did not realize existed or that they were trying to ignore or sweep under the rug for the time being. Help them to understand the consequences of doing so, along with the extended costs. Show them how putting a solution like yours in place will make a difference in their output, revenue, and productivity and how they will be seen as the hero for implementing a solution with such a positive impact on the company. This will help them see the need. Be patient with your prospect during this stage and use a little bit of finesse. If they are meant to work with you and your company, they will come around, but don't stronghold them.

I'm happy with my current solution. When the prospect tells you they are happy with their current solution, you must strike a delicate balance not to bash your competition. Have the prospect go over the things they like about their current solution. Once they've told you what they do like, ask them if there is anything they'd like to see improved. This will crack open the door for you to discuss a possible solution that can bridge this gap for them. Again, approach this carefully. If they told you that they like their current provider, you don't want to paint them in a negative light. You simply want to open the door for them to consider alternative solutions.

Lack of urgency. You can't force a prospect to act on your own timeline, but you can evaluate whether or not they can benefit from having your solution in place sooner rather than later. Oftentimes, when there is a lack of urgency, the prospect has acknowledged that there is a need, and they see some value in your solution but not enough to take action. They are still in the passive stage of the buying process. You can move them to the active stage by helping them to see what the outcome would be should they ignore or put off taking action. For example, depending on the solution, it is possible that letting their existing problem continue to develop will cost them more money in the long run to fix than it would if they took the proactive approach and started working on it now. How much is it worth to your prospect to save considerable dollars in their budget by getting ahead of the problem rather than allow it to fester?

Lack of authority. If you have not been diligent in getting the decision maker involved in the process, it is possible that you will get further into your sales process only to discover that your primary contact does not have the authority to make decisions. I hope this doesn't happen often, but if it does, work with your contact to try and set up a meeting with the decision maker to move the process forward. Don't rely on them to relay the message and share the information without your presence. Insist on being there. After all, you are the expert on the matter and will be able to answer any questions the decision maker has about the solution. Stroke your contact's ego by letting them know the accolades they will receive from their boss by implementing such a solution that will solve the company's problems and ultimately save them money, time and resources.

Time. A common objection you may receive from a prospect is that they don't have time to work on this project. They may claim not to have the time to implement it and babysit it through the process to see the results you are claiming. Counter this by asking them what the anticipated results would mean to them. How much of an impact would it make on them and their business to implement your solution? Forget the time involved to implement it. If they could skip through to the end result, what would that mean to them? If you get a positive response and your prospect can still see the value in it, perhaps suggest that they appoint a project manager to work with you through the project while they oversee it. Help them to review their current resources to see the best way for them to implement your solution with a minimal time investment on their end.

I'll get back to you. This is a common objection that sales professionals often receive and at the time, they don't even realize that it's an objection. That is, until the prospect stops returning your calls. Don't let your prospect off the hook when you have them engaged. Instead of settling for "I'll get back to you," put a date on the calendar when that will happen. Schedule a time to meet with the prospect or call them with a specific goal and agenda to move the process forward. Take initiative for what you will bring to the table at the next meeting but also assign some responsibility to the prospect as well to make them more accountable.

I could spend all day going over the various forms of objections that your prospect will throw your way. The key is being prepared. You will not enter into a sales call without any objections. Don't think of it as negative; rather, consider it part of the sales process. The prospect is doing their due diligence by putting these obstacles in front of you. The way you handle them will determine the type of relationship you build with them moving forward.

Take the time to understand and empathize with their objection, no matter what it is. Never dismiss it. That is a quick way out of the door. Instead, show them that you relate to their feelings and share with them how the solution that you're offering is more of a benefit than a deterrent. Use every opportunity to educate the prospect on their needs and how you can help meet them.

When your prospect feels that you understand them and their concerns, they are more likely to allow you to move along to the next step in the process.

B.U.D. STRATEGY FOR DEALING WITH OBJECTIONS

BETTER: Expect your prospect to object. It is a natural part of the sales process and as a professional, you should be prepared to address any of their concerns by being armed with their goals and intentions and using that as ammunition to dispel their concerns.

UNIQUE: Address the objections, even if your prospect doesn't. It's not opening up a can of worms. Instead, you are getting into your prospect's head again to address their concerns and set them at ease about making a choice to work with you.

DESIRABLE: Empathize with and understand their concerns. Don't get overworked or offended by anything they say. Use it as an opportunity to educate your prospect and reiterate their needs so that you can serve them in the best possible way.

CHAPTER 9: FOLLOW UP

Follow up is one of the most integral components in the sales process. No prospect makes a decision to accept your product or service the first day you walk through their doors or pick up the phone. It requires persistent effort, and this is where follow up comes in.

One of the key mistakes sales professionals make is simply giving up too soon. There are going to be sales that close very quickly with little effort but there are also going to be those that require consistent follow up to achieve your goal.

When it comes to marketing messages, it is common knowledge that it takes at least seven times for a person to hear that message before it registers, or they take action. Use this as a test when you are in the follow up process with your prospect. Never assume that you are bothering the prospect by simply communicating with them on a consistent basis. Follow your prospect's queue when it comes to follow up. Find out the way they like to communicate and use that method. Ask them if it's okay to follow up on a weekly, monthly basis to check the status of their process. Prospects can be fickle when it comes to making decisions. They could tell you today that they are not looking to make a change and change their mind in a few months when you check in with them. However, if you don't have time scheduled to follow up with them, you may miss out on an opportunity to close a sale.

This is why I adapted the part of my B.U.D. philosophy that I call pleasantly persistent. By staying in regular communication with your customer, you can ensure that you stay top of mind when they are finally ready to make a decision. Don't take yourself out of the loop. One of the keys to staying pleasantly persistent is to diversify your communication so that it never becomes stale, and it doesn't feel like you're saying the same thing every time you reach out to them. I've broken down this process into seven steps. Let's review them.

1. ***Begin your process with an introductory email.*** This is an easy way to start your communication with your prospect as email is considered noninvasive. You are more likely to receive a quick response from a prospect via email rather than by phone because most people have access to their emails even when they are on the go and are more likely to respond in a timely manner. When developing your email, you want to be creative and devise a crafty or eye-catching subject line that will capture the attention of your prospect. Chances are, they receive a considerable number of emails on a daily basis so while the chances are higher that they may respond more quickly to your email over your call, you want to create something engaging that will prompt a response. This goes back to understanding their needs and what clicks with them. Put yourself in their shoes and imagine what would engage them.

2. ***Follow up your email with a phone call.*** Now that you have established communication with your prospect via email, the next step is to engage with them over the phone. You have them on the hook now so you're no stranger to them when you place the phone call. Make sure you reference the email when you make the phone call to capture their interest and attention. This call should be made 3-5 days after your first email.

3. *Follow up with your phone call with a second email.* In the email, reference what was discussed in the first email to remind the prospect of pertinent information.

4. *Follow up your second email with a second phone call.* By this step, you should be 10-12 days into the process. Don't rush it. Just follow the formula. Remember, we're being pleasantly persistent which means we don't want to be banging on their door and calling them every single day. Give them time to receive and process the information that you are providing them before moving on to the next step.

5. *Send pertinent articles of interest to your prospect.* This shakes the process up a little bit and shows the prospect that you are studying them and have an active interest in their business and what they do. This is more the move of a consultant instead of a sales representative because it is not a move that is designed to make them take action and buy your product. Instead, what it is doing is inspiring trust. They see that you care about their business and what they care about, and it begins to break down the barrier between them and yourself, opening the door for a relationship.

6. *Find your prospect on social media and like or comment on their posts.* Be authentic in your communication. A prospect can spot a fake a mile away so seek opportunities to make genuine comments about what they are posting. If you notice posts on social medida that you think would appeal to them, share it with them or tag them, much like the articles that you sent in step 5. Your goal here is to let them

know that you are paying attention and care about what they are doing.

7. ***Send the prospect a unique or funny card.*** This step is meant to take things a little lightly and begin to establish some sort of relationship with them. Let them know you have a sense of humor. Make them laugh, and then repeat the process again. Your goal in these communications is not to initiate an immediate sale; it's to build a relationship.

The more you engage with your prospect and practice my pleasantly persistent method, the more likely you are to be top of mind when they are ready to make a buying decision. This process of follow up can last a few months to a few years, depending upon the prospect, but all that matters is that you don't give up. The more you engage with your entire pipeline on this level, the more success you will have.

AFTER THE SALE

Once the sale is made, you don't want to abandon the process of being pleasantly persistent with your new customer. It is important that you continue to stay engaged with your new customer. After all, why would you have gone through all that trouble of building the relationship just to abandon your new customer once the sale is closed? Your new customer is just as valuable, if not more valuable once the sale is closed. The more you nurture and build that new relationship, the more customers are willing to do for you, making your job much easier. The last thing you want is a revolving door of customers because you failed to follow through once you gained their trust.

We will get into this in one of the next chapters but one of the skills a sales professional can develop is their ability to nurture their customers and drive referrals. The best sales representatives have learned how to turn their customers into their raving fans and their own personal sales force. The result is that they have to do much less cold calling and prospecting to grow their pipeline. Can you imagine that for your own business? Then, master the art of follow up and being pleasantly persistent throughout the life cycle of your customer.

KNOW YOUR COMPETITION

You wouldn't necessarily think that the competition is part of your sales process, but you need to know what you're up against no matter who your competition is. There is this mantra to keep blinders on when you're running a race and in some cases that makes sense, but even the professional football players watch tape of their competition before every game. They search for their strengths and weaknesses so that they can build a winning strategy. The same is true when it comes to evaluating your competition.

Just as it is important for you to study your prospects and your customers, you should also take the time to study your competition. Know who is good at what so that you are armed with this information when you meet with your customers. You never want to fly in blind because some of your prospects will quiz you on what their current provider is offering to compare. At the end of the day, you want to focus on how you can create an optimal experience for your prospect and fill the gap or deficiency that you know your competitor embodies.

How do you do this?

Customer Service. Always provide value to show your customer why they should do business with you. As I mentioned earlier in this book, you never want to get into a price war with your prospect or your competition. What are you able to give your customer that no one else can? What problems can you solve? What is your unique selling proposition? Go above and beyond to provide your prospect excellent customer service, not just through the sales process, but post sales as well. Continue to prove to your customer that you are trustworthy and good for your word.

Be Better. Strive for a standard of excellence in everything you do. Don't just seek to meet your prospect's expectations, but rather, to exceed them. Seek to be the best at what you do. If that means investing in your education and working overtime to learn everything there is to learn about your prospect and their business, do it.

Be Unique. When we were little kids, you were considered weird if you were different or stood out. As an adult, it is encouraged and praised. After all, no one person is truly alike. Ask yourself what you bring to the table for your prospect or customer that no one else can. There is nothing wrong with thinking out of the box to solve a problem for a client. Don't adopt the mantra of 'that's the way we've always done it.' There are always new and innovative ways to serve your customers and meet their needs.

B.U.D. STRATEGY FOR FOLLOW UP

BETTER: *Don't give up too soon. Keep your foot on the pedal. Stay persistent.*

UNIQUE: Be pleasantly persistent throughout the follow up process. Every touch point does not have to be the same. Shake things up. Follow the B.U.D. formula for follow up.

DESIRABLE: Stay actively engaged with your prospect throughout the process and it will never seem as if you're bothering them. In fact, they will come to expect and look forward to your communication.

CASE STUDY: FOLLOW UP

PATRICK

Patrick and I have been working together strategically for quite some time. He is a marketing professional and I'm a sales coach so what we do complements each other. Naturally, we tend to rub off on one another, which I would chalk up to iron sharpening iron.

A valuable lesson Patrick learned at one of my training sessions was the value of using your proposal to your advantage to further build the relationship with your prospect and keep your foot in the door. Patrick had gotten into that song and dance with the prospect where he'd prepare a proposal and email it to the prospect and then try to follow up to get their attention and discuss. He was losing a lot of opportunities following this process as a lot of prospects fell into that black hole where you never heard from them again. I taught him to never email the proposal to the prospect and wait to hear back from them. Rather, you want to schedule a call or a meeting to go over the proposal with them. This ensures that you get back in front of them to keep moving the sales process forward.

Another thing Patrick learned in my training session is to refer to your proposal as a working document. For some reason, prospects see a proposal as final and when they know there is room for adaptation and changes, they are more open to what you have to share. In their mind, when they hear proposal, I think they relate it to contract, meaning it can't be updated and it can't be changed. By using the term working document, you are assuring them that you are working through solutions to determine what is best for their company, much more customer centric. Also, when scheduling that appointment to review the proposal, I taught Patrick that if the customer is not willing to set that meeting with you to go over that information, you don't move forward. You learn a lot about your relationship and where the customer is in the buying process by how they respond here. When they are ready to move to the next level of the sales process, they will schedule that appointment with you. Otherwise, you rule them out as a prospect or revisit the opportunity with them at a later time when it is more relevant and more of a priority for them.

These small nuggets saved Patrick time and money because he didn't waste time working with prospects that were not serious about moving forward with him.

CHAPTER 10: CLOSING

As important as it is to nurture the customer and build a relationship, you don't invest all of this time and energy never to ask for the sale. One of the pivotal mistakes that sales representatives make is assuming the customer will close themself. News flash, they won't. You have to ask for the sale and guide the prospect through the buying process.

Here are a few things to consider when guiding your prospect through the closing process.

In a previous chapter, we talked about your unique selling proposition. What is your special sauce that makes you and your company unique? Why would your prospect want to do business with you? During the closing process, you want to remind your prospect why they want to do business with you. Tell them how your customized solution can solve their problem and how you are uniquely qualified to get them to the finish line.

Concentrate on your prospect's expectations. It's not about your agenda or what you want to accomplish. Remember that you are there to help your prospect achieve their goals and objectives, not your own. Keep the focus on them.

Devise a solution that is specific to the needs of your prospect. Again, remember not to satisfy your own selfish ambitions, even if that means you take a smaller commission because it's a smaller sale. If you've done your homework and followed the guidelines I've outlined in this book, you will have prepared a solution that will speak to exactly what your prospect needs, no matter how big or small. Taking the time to nurture the relationship and focus on their needs will result in a long-term relationship that will yield dividends in your future.

Have you ever heard that you have two ears and one mouth for a reason? Zip your lips and listen to your prospect. They will tell you exactly what you need to hear to answer their needs. All you need to do is simply listen.

Under promise and overdeliver. Listen to what your prospect needs and go above and beyond their expectations.

Continue to wow them by showing your interest in them and their company by the research you've done beforehand. Show them that they are not just a number to you.

When you are working to close a sale, review the benefits after your sales presentation. You've already established the needs of your prospect by asking the right questions. Now it is time to move them to action. Reiterating their pain points and how you will solve them is the perfect recap to this process.

The trial close is the perfect way to identify any objections and address them after you have presented a solution to their problem. During the trial close, you will have clear yes and no questions to identify whether or not there are any issues with the solution you have presented. If you are getting clear yes's during the trial close, that is a key indication that your prospect is ready to move on to the commitment stage. If you start to receive 'no's, that means you need to do a little more detective work to identify where the roadblocks might be. This doesn't mean that you can't close the sale. It simply means you need to ask more questions and get more clarity on what the prospect wants and/or needs.

Here is an example to illustrate how this close would work:

Salesperson: Do you feel this training program will meet all of your needs?
Prospect: Yes, when can we get started?

In this scenario, your prospect has given you a clear signal that they are ready to move forward.

Salesperson: Do you feel this training program will meet all of your needs?
Prospect: It is an impressive program. I like what you have to offer.

In this scenario, it is clear that your prospect has concerns that they are not revealing. Ask more questions to get to the root of the problem and find out what is preventing them from saying yes.

The assumptive close is another technique you can use during the closing process. In this case, you confidently assume the client is ready to move to the next level of the sales process. The assumptive close is a more direct approach and requires a bold, confident stance to execute it efficiently.

Salesperson: It looks like we've been able to meet all of your needs based on what we've discussed. Why don't we schedule your project for next Wednesday?

While examining different techniques is helpful when you are closing sales, taking a one-thousand-foot view of the process often provides more perspective to make your techniques more effective. Let's dive a little deeper into the emotional intelligence of closing the sale.

Don't allow yourself to make excuses. It is our natural inclination to blame someone or something else when things are not going the way we planned. This includes our performance when it comes to closing the sale. One of the best things you can do for yourself if you find your performance slipping is to take responsibility. Ask yourself why you have fallen short of meeting your goal. Why were you not able to finish? Did you actually attempt to close the sale, or did you leave it to the prospect to close the sale for you? Did you ask the right questions to uncover the prospect's true need? Did you allow the prospect's objections to get in the way of your close? There are many variables to why you didn't close that sale or why your performance might have been lacking. Without taking a step back to examine yourself, and your process, you will never get to the real answers. So, always be accountable for your actions, good or bad. Even when things are going well and you find that you are closing more sales, ask yourself the same questions so that you can learn what you're doing well to duplicate it in the future.

Remember that your prospect has the answers you need. Earlier in the book, we talked about being prepared and doing your due diligence before your meeting with the customer. A lot of information about their company and background can be gleaned from conducting this research, but you will never learn more than what that prospect is willing to share with you. However, they are not going to just volunteer this information. As the sales professional, you must play the role of detective to learn this information. Never tire of asking good questions to the prospect to uncover more about their needs. Just when you think you've asked enough questions, ask more. Your prospect has the answers to everything you need.

Stay focused. There will always be plenty of distractions to throw you off track from achieving your goal. Always know what you are trying to accomplish. Life is busy and distractions will compete for your attention. The truth is all distractions are not bad. However, when you walk into the appointment with that prospect, you want to give them 100% of your focus. Clear your mind before walking into the appointment so that you can give them your full attention. Depending on what may be going on at the time, this can be difficult, I know. But your prospect deserves your full attention, and if you intend to win their business, you cannot afford to give them anything less.

Don't rely too heavily on technology. Technology is a tool designed to make us more effective; however, too often, it has become a crutch. Here's a good example - think of one of your closest friends or family members that you talk to on a regular basis. What is their cell phone number? Chances are, you don't know it, because you have come to rely on the address book in your cell phone to store it. That's how we've come to use technology as a crutch and that is on a very basic level. That being said, it is important to understand that sales are based on relationships. Don't be afraid to pick up the phone to talk to your prospect. While email and text messages are efficient ways to communicate, they should not be our primary means of communication with our prospect. Video calls have become more common in the business world as we have learned to adapt to a new way of communicating. Making use of these is an example of using technology to your advantage rather than a crutch. The goal when using technology is to always use it to enhance what you are doing with the prospect, not necessarily replace it. Nothing will ever replace the human connection. As long as you remember that, you will continue to build relationships and close more sales.

Choose quality prospects. When building your list and choosing the prospects to go after, you should be judicious. All prospects are not a good fit for your business and what you are looking for. When preparing your prospect list, you should ask yourself who your ideal customer is and why? When you know the answers to these questions, you can narrow down your list of prospects to companies that fit your needs. Observe patterns in your sales process to determine if you are choosing the right prospects for your business. If you are running into the same objections or challenges over and over again, you need to re-evaluate your process. Yes, it is possible that you need to course correct in other areas of your sales process, such as the questions you're asking, but it is also possible that you are going after the wrong prospects. Make sure the prospects you are choosing have a need for the product or service that you're offering; otherwise, you're going to have a difficult time making the sale. You are not going to sell everyone anyway. A good closing ratio for an excellent sales professional is between 25 - 30%. That means 70-75% of the time, you are not going to close the sale. With that knowledge in hand, you want to make sure that the integrity of your prospect list is strong because the last thing you want to do is chase a poor prospect down the rabbit hole only to discover they were never a good fit for you in the first place. This goes back to one of the key fundamentals we discussed at the beginning of the book about being prepared. It is better to spend more time on the front end of the process preparing a strong prospect list than to waste your time going after prospects that will never close.

Never take your customers for granted. One of the biggest mistakes sales professionals make is resting on their laurels after they make the sale. Why would you compromise the sale you worked so hard to make? The relationship with your new customer is just beginning. The last thing you want to do is abandon it once they finally say yes. This is a key moment of trust in the process. Your new customer is waiting to see if you are good for your word. They want to know if they were just a number to you or if you care about helping them solve their problems. Failure to follow through after the sale is made will not only affect the longevity of your new customer, but any future business you might have gleaned from that relationship by simply serving them. Continue to nurture that new relationship with your customer and show them why they should continue doing business with you; otherwise, they won't.

Don't use price to make the sale. If you rely on price to close your sale, you have already lost. You never want to get into this battle with your prospect. It is your responsibility to show value. Even if your prospect touts the importance of price, it will never be the sole reason for them to do business with you. Regardless of their cost sensitivity, the most important thing to your prospect is that you solve their problem, that you are answering a need. Coming in at the lowest price but coming up short in meeting the prospect's needs will always be short lived. If you want to build a relationship with the prospect that is long term, focus on how you are going to serve those needs long term and what it will mean to them, beyond price. Focus on your value proposition to help the prospect see why they should do business with you, even if your price is higher than your competitors.

It is still important to sell your company. While we talk about selling yourself throughout the sales process, it is still important to sell your company. After all, that is who they are ultimately doing business with. It is true that your prospect will build trust in you first. But that trust then needs to extend to trust in your company and what it is able to deliver to meet their needs. You have the responsibility of communicating that to the prospect to make them feel comfortable with the new partnership they are forging. In order for the prospect to see this, it needs to shine through you. That means you need to show your trust in your company and its ability to meet the prospect's needs. You need to believe that your company can follow through on all of your promises. If you do not have that same trust in your company, it can easily show through to your prospect, compromising your sale and your relationship.

A good sales professional also needs to see through the lens of the prospect or the customer to understand how they are thinking and how they are perceiving them through the process. The better understanding you have of what your prospect sees or understands, the better your chances of closing the sale.

A recent study conducted on sales professionals showed that prospects rank the attitude of the sales professional higher than aptitude and know-how.[1] With this in mind, consider how your prospect is ranking you. What characteristics are you exhibiting, and do you need to pivot or change your attitude to alter your prospect's perception of you?

Jaded. If the prospect sees you as jaded, they don't have a positive perception of you. The jaded sales professional has a glass half-empty attitude. They focus on the problem over the solution and tend to have more of a skeptical or cynical attitude. It is easy for the prospect to see their lack of interest because they make no effort to really hide it. You don't want your prospect to see you in this category because it will clearly compromise your ability to connect and close the sale.

Jobber. The jobber is a good little soldier. While they are not jaded, they see their position as a job and nothing more. They clock in from 9-5 and at 5:01, they are done. The jobber takes very little risks. They follow the rules and don't rock the boat. They want to stay within the lines, do their job and nothing else. You will not find a jobber going above and beyond the call of duty. If it was up to them, they'd probably be doing something else with the company.

Jazzed. The jazzed sales professional is high energy. They love their job, and they are fully committed to achievement. They are magnetic and their energy is infectious. They are the stark opposite of the jaded professional. They are always excited about the opportunity that lies before them,

---

[1] Nanji, A. (n.d.) *The 10 Sales Behaviors That Are Deal-Breakers for B2B Buyers.* Marketing Profs. Retrieved Dec. 13, 2021: https://www.marketingprofs.com/charts/2021/46245/the-10-sales-behaviors-that-are-deal-breakers-for-b2b-buyers

and it shows with their prospects. They are always eager to learn, interact and develop new relationships. Unlike the jobber, they are never satisfied with where they are. They always want to take it to the next level, always seeking a challenge and going above and beyond to achieve their goals and serve the needs of their customers and prospects. They are persistent in the face of adversity, and it doesn't scare them. They push when many would quit. They always see the light at the end of the tunnel. A jazzed sales professional is always going to fight for you.

While each of these descriptions seem a bit extreme, it is important to know that prospects are evaluating sales professionals on that scale, and they will see you as one of the three. Of course, the jazzed sales professional will achieve more sales because they are the most committed of the three. That does not mean that the jaded or jobber never makes sales, but they will never achieve the level of success of the jazzed sales professional.

B.U.D. STRATEGY FOR CLOSING

BETTER: Ask for the sale. Don't spend all of your time cultivating your relationship and working through the sales process only to stall at the end.

UNIQUE: Know how the prospect perceives you. Study the different attitudes that prospects put sales professionals in and ask yourself what bucket you fall into. If you discover that your attitude is undesirable, make a change and course correct with your prospect.

DESIRABLE: Stay focused on your prospect and their needs. All communication should be funneled through their needs and solving their problems. As long as you remember that it's not about you, you are on the right track.

CASE STUDY: CLOSING

DENNIS

Dennis worked as an operations executive for his company where he was able to create breakthrough results in revenue during his tenure. As a result, he was asked to take over the management of the company's sales team. Realizing that sales was not an area he was familiar with, he sought leadership and training to assist him in meeting his company goals.

Dennis and I worked together to define the sales process and evaluate his current sales team to determine benchmarks. Dennis had 10 sales representatives in place and over the first year, we worked together to evaluate his team to learn everyone's capacities, strengths and weaknesses. Based on each assessment, we were able to identify those strengths and weaknesses and capitalize accordingly.

We worked together to build a sales program to maximize the capacity and productivity of the sales team. Over the next 5 years, the team was able to help the company reach its goal of $51 million in revenue. Dennis credits my training and coaching as being instrumental in helping him achieve a successful result. By setting goals, boundaries, and reward systems, he was able to build an effective team.

CHAPTER 11: NURTURING THE CUSTOMER

We touched on this a little bit in the last chapter, but it bears repeating. The sales process does not end once you land the customer. In fact, it is just beginning. You have taken the time and effort to earn that new customer; now, you must do the work to keep them. A lot of sales professionals stop their efforts once they win the sale, thinking their work is done once they've won the business. Taking the time to nurture your customers and develop them into your raving fans is what will separate you from your competition and put you among the cream of the crop as a sales professional.

Here is an interesting statistic to help you understand why it is so important to keep and nurture that new customer you just worked so hard for: Recent studies reveal that it will cost you five times more money to get a new customer than what it will cost to keep an existing customer. Therefore, simply increasing your customer retention as little as 5% can increase your company profits a minimum of 25%. While a big part of your job as a sales professional might be to get new business, why not work smarter rather than harder? Taking the time to nurture and cultivate your existing customers will not only lead to additional opportunities within that account, but referral opportunities as well. As an elite sales professional, you must learn the delicate balance of mining your own prospects and building existing relationships to create new ones. If you ever thought sales was a one-dimensional role, you are seriously mistaken. To own your position as a great sales professional, you must learn how to balance multiple plates and do it well.

When it comes to cultivating sales with your existing customers, consider this your low hanging fruit in your business. You don't have to break through the barrier of gaining trust like you do in a new relationship. Your existing customers already see you as a consultant and trusted expert in what you do. Therefore, they are likely to follow your lead when it comes to your recommendations for their business. Also, because you've done your homework in learning their business and their needs, you are going to be more intuitive when it comes to products and services that will benefit them the most.

Let's explore some ways to dive in and take advantage of more business within your existing accounts.

- ***Study your accounts.*** Like you study your new prospects when you are starting a new relationship, continue to study your new customers. Keep a file or make notes in your CRM system as you uncover new information as it pertains to their specific needs or changes in their business. Review the things they told you from the outset of their business with them along with subsequent conversations and uncover potential opportunities to discuss with them. Ask yourself, how can you serve them better? What more can you offer them to make their lives and business easier? Looking at additional opportunities might lie beyond your current point of contact with this customer. Perhaps there might be other opportunities to implement your product or service in other departments or branches of their business. Do your homework to discover how you might be able to pitch this, and then schedule an appointment with your customer to discuss how you might discuss possible solutions with their colleagues.

- *Research their challenges.* As you are doing your research to uncover opportunities with your company, observe any recurring trends. Is the problem they seem to be having consistent within their industry or is there a deficiency within their system that is causing it? Dig deep to find the source of their problem and why so that you can provide a more comprehensive solution. As you're doing your research, consider their current providers and the current relationship they have with them. As always, you don't ever want to bash the competition, but you do want to discover their deficiencies and where they are not meeting your customer's needs and why. Use this as an opening to discover more about their challenges and how you might be able to fill the gaps in their product or service.

- *Put together a plan.* Once you've done your research and learned the challenges your customer is experiencing, you want to develop a customized plan to solve these challenges.

- *Ask for an introduction.* Now that you have a plan to present to your customer, leverage your relationship with your main contact to introduce you to the department leaders or branch managers that you are targeting to share your plan. As mentioned earlier, you want to start this process by having a meeting with your main contact first to let them know that you'd like to expand your business within their company. Let them know how much you value your relationship with them and the business that you've built. Focus on how you've been able to help them solve problems and make improvements in their business processes and how you feel you can do the same for their colleagues. Share with them the research you've done on their other departments so they can see that you've made an effort to do your homework and that you're not relying solely on them to do it for you. Show them that you have a vested interest in their success and that you'd like to partner together to provide a solution for them.

It's really as simple as that. Ask for the introduction. Leverage your relationship with your customer, while also showing appreciation for their business. Focus on the solution for their colleagues, just as you focused on the solution for them. Stay consistent in showing your customer that you care about their business and making their lives easier. As long as you continue to be honest and authentic in your approach, your customer will open the door for you to grow your business with them again and again.

As you seek to grow your relationship with your existing customers, you don't want it to be one-sided. Don't put yourself in a position where your customer starts to feel as if you are always trying to get something from them. You need to earn the right to ask for business from them and continue to build trust. You do this by continuing to serve them and letting them know you have their best interest at heart. Show them that you appreciate their business by taking an active interest in theirs. Fight against the stereotype that sales professionals are selfish and only out to reach their own ambitions. Show them that you genuinely care about their business, even if you don't get anything directly from it.

- *Seek to add value.* Always look to add value to the relationship. Ask yourself what you can do to make their lives easier. Since you've taken the time to learn their business and understand their hot buttons, introduce them to potential customers to grow their own business as you encounter them. Let them know that you are not only interested in growing your business but theirs as well.

- *Help them find strategic partners.* Part of the reason why you are leveraging yourself as a consultant over a salesperson is so that you can work alongside your customer as a partner. As you've come to understand their business, you are more familiar with the components that will contribute to their success. Brainstorm ideas and share with them ways to boost their revenue and help them form strategic partnerships that will further elevate their market share. The more you openly share this information with your customers, the more they will begin to look to you as a resource to help them grow their business.

- *Show direct interest.* Remember, everything does not have to be about business all the time. You are building a relationship and that means just being friendly and going the extra mile sometimes. Take the time to learn your customers' birthdays. Send them a card or flowers on their birthday. Send them a card at Christmas. Learn about what is important to them, whether it's their family or their dog. Ask about those things when you speak with them. Show them that you care. Be genuine. People will do business with people that they like.

Part of the nurturing process is ensuring that your customers stay with you. Remember the cost to acquire a new customer? And, while that might be part of your process, you don't want to be in the business of continually replacing existing customers. You want to retain the customers you have and then continue to grow from there. But how do you maximize your retention with your customers?

- ***Give your customers a reason to return.*** Depending upon your product or service, you might have to service the customer, or the initial sale might be transactional. Either way, you want to create an experience where the customer wants to keep coming back to you. No matter what stage you are in the sales process, never get overconfident. You could reason that the customer needs you, but don't ever forget that they always have a choice. You have a responsibility to make sure that choice continues to be you, and that decision will be dictated by how you treat them. As I mentioned earlier, you need to show them that you care. Give them the best possible experience they can have with you and your company.

- ***Set realistic expectation levels.*** In the beginning you want to set reasonable expectations with your customers about your role and theirs as your relationship matures. Anytime you are able to exceed those expectations and go above and beyond, you are further solidifying your relationship with your new customer.

- ***Be good for your word.*** If you promised something to your customer during the sales process, don't abandon it once they say yes. You have an obligation to fulfill your promises to your customer because they are counting on you to be good for your word. Remember when you are just getting started, you are still in the honeymoon phase of your relationship. That means that your new customer is testing to see if you are truly good for your word or if you fall into the negative stereotype of the salesperson who over-promises and under-delivers. Deliver your promise to your customer and then "wow" them by doing just a little bit more.

- **_Understand your customer._** We talked about this a bit already, but you need to take the time to get to know your customer and their business so that they know and understand that you care about more than just your own bottom line. They need to understand that you care about improving their business. Seek to build a true, genuine relationship with your customers and they'll never want to leave you.

How do you continue to go the extra mile when it comes to retaining your customers? Let's observe one of the best examples of customer service in the food and retail industries - Chick-fil-a. They make a point to delight their customers at every turn, all the way to their signature phrase, "my pleasure." Their signature touch is meant to demonstrate to their customers that they value doing business with them. Nordstrom seeks to delight their customers by simple acts like walking around the counter to hand their bags to their customers instead of handing it across the counter. It's that little extra that counts, which moves these companies one notch above their competitors.

What small things do you think that you can incorporate into your interactions with your customers to yield the same results as truly successful companies?

- ***Don't take your relationship for granted.*** Once you've established trust with your new customer, it is easy to take our foot off the gas and take this relationship for granted. You should always be investing in the growth of your relationship with your customer. As you develop trust and mature the relationship, you don't necessarily need to do as much as you did at the outset of the relationship when you were trying to earn their business. At the same time, you never want to just abandon your customer either. Always keep your finger on the pulse. Stay top of mind with your customer at all times; otherwise, someone else will come in and occupy their mind and you definitely don't want that to happen. Continue to provide an experience for your customer that will keep them coming back for more.

- ***You don't need a reason to contact your customer.*** Don't reserve your communication with your customer for times when they need something or when you need something. One of the most valuable ways to build and solidify your relationship with your customer is the times you contact them for no apparent reason at all. Just like you value the 'just because' in a romantic relationship, your customer does as well. Taking the time to check in on them to see how they're doing and how you can better serve them not only puts you above your competition, but it further shows them how much you value them and your relationship.

- ***Compliment your customer.*** No two customers are alike. There must be some things that you admire about working with your customer, whether it is their business model or the way they organize their processes. Take the time to compliment them on the things you admire about them and what they do. Let them know how much you enjoy working with them. A little bit always goes a long way. You don't know what kind of day they may have been having and simply offering a compliment to let them know how much you appreciate them might just be the bright spot in their day.

- *Ask for feedback.* One of your goals should always be to leverage yourself as a partner with your customer. You want them to be able to lean on you when they need something, even if it does not directly pertain to the service or product that you offer. Open the door for them by asking for direct feedback from your customer. Ask what you do to ease their workload. How can you make working for them easier? Show them that you are always seeking to improve and grow and to do that, you need their direct feedback.

- *Offer improvements where you think it will benefit their business.* Relationships are a two-way street. Just as you seek their feedback to improve the service that you offer them, offer your own feedback to your customers to help improve their processes or their operation. Always be observant and look for ways to serve your customer. It doesn't matter if your suggestion has anything to do with your company, product, or service, or not. Simply the fact that you are observant enough to take an active interest in their business will further ground your relationship with your customer.

- *Be a problem solver.* Let's face it, things are not always going to operate smoothly throughout your relationship. There are going to be bumps in the road. People are going to screw up, whether it's you or someone in your company. Mistakes happen. What matters is how you respond to them. That is what your customer is waiting to see. They want to see how you handle situations that are less than ideal. The best way to handle mistakes or mishaps is to simply be honest with your customer. Communicate with them how you will solve the problem at hand and put them at ease. Let them know they are in good hands with you because you will not let them down.

- *Take your customer complaints seriously.* There may be times when a customer complaint seems petty to you, but to them, it may be a big deal. Don't trivialize it. Take them seriously and let them know that you are going to take care of them and their problem. Gaining the trust of your customer with the small things will almost certainly assure you that they will trust you when you have to solve a big challenge for them.

Now that you're vested in cultivating a strong relationship with your customers, how do you make them your raving fans? The happiest and most satisfied customers will become your external sales force, working with you to keep your pipeline full. What are some things you can do to get your customers more involved in your sales process, above and beyond what we've just discussed?

- *Exceed expectations.* This should go without saying and I don't want to beat a dead horse here, but the more you delight and please your customers, the more they are going to want to return the favor. A customer that is happy with your service and the work that you're doing will happily refer you to their friends before you even open your mouth to ask.

- **Consider a customer loyalty program.** While this may take more time and effort to put in place, customers love to be rewarded for their actions. Your loyalty program can be as complex as a point-based system with different prizes to something as simple as free or discounted services for every new customer they refer. Be as creative as you want when conjuring up ideas for this. You might even consider surveying your customers to get their direct feedback on what would motivate them to participate more actively in referrals. History has shown that you always get some of your best ideas and feedback from them. Plus, they will appreciate the fact that you value their opinion and that you are including them in your process.

- **Stay engaged with your customers.** We have said this several times in this book but that is because it is extremely important if you value the relationship with your customers and all of the work you did to get them. If you keep track of your sales in a CRM, I encourage you to continue to set dates for follow up with your customer after the sale has been completed. Remember to also include those "just because" calls or visits to check in with them. You never want to take your finger off the pulse with your customers. Always make an effort to show them how much you care and that you haven't dropped the ball because you made the sale.

- **Provide your customer with a template for referrals.** If you are going to ask your customer to refer business to you, make it easy for them. While they might appreciate what you do and are happy to share it with others, they are not a salesperson. Provide a template that will outline the basic information they'd need to share for a referral. A plug and play model will make it easy for your customer to help you and share with their colleagues and friends.

- *Use stories to make their experience shareable.* You want to give your customers a good reason to refer business to you. Part of that reason is their own personal experience working with you, but you can enrich that by providing other case studies of companies that have worked with you and what their outcome have been. Not only does that give your customer ammunition to refer more business to you, but it further renews their trust in you and your company and what you are able to offer and deliver to your customers. Offering stories and case studies gets your customer excited about sharing with their friends and colleagues. You've already established a level of belief and trust through your own relationship but learning what you have done for others renews that belief even more.

- *Use social media as a tool to drive referrals.* We discussed LinkedIn and other tools for prospecting at another section of this book, but it is also an excellent tool for researching leads for referrals. Use the search tools within the platform to identify prospects that you'd like to connect with. If you have mutual connections, such as one of your customers, ask that person for an introduction to kick off your communication.

- **_Offer incentives._** While this option is similar to putting a customer referral program in place, it is a bit more informal and easier to manage on your part. An incentive could be something as simple as offering a gift card to your customer for referring business to you. An even better way to incentivize your customer is to know what they like and offer that. If you know they love ice cream, offer them a gift card to an ice cream shoppe. If you know they like the outdoors, offer them a gift card to a sporting goods store. Make it personal and this will continue to build on and solidify your relationship with your customer.

- **_Choose the right timing._** If you had a difficult onboarding process with your new customer, it would hardly make sense to ask for a referral at that time. You want to choose an opportunity where your customer is experiencing something positive to ask for the referral. It should never be a forced endeavor.

- **_Seek opportunities for advocacy._** Don't get offended if your customer says no when you ask for a referral. You want this experience to be genuine and you want to give your customer the time and space to want to offer this to you. Instead of pushing, just take a step back and give your customer the time and space they need. Continue to serve them and create an amazing experience for them, affirming with them that you are not relying on them to do something for you in order for you to return the favor. When some time has gone by and you feel comfortable approaching them again, consider a different approach. Instead of asking for a referral, why not approach them this time and ask for a testimonial or case study revealing a good experience they've had with you. Participating in these smaller activities will still yield leads for you and your company, while allowing you to continue to build trust in your new customer relationship. As you continue to give your customer more time, you may find that they offer to give you that referral you were asking for all on their own.

- *Know your customer's values.* This goes back to doing your homework which has been reiterated over and over in this book. Know what is important to your customer. Study your customer. Go on their website and read about their mission and their values. For example, if you find that your customer is very involved in the community and civic action, offer to help them organize an event to support their cause. Align with them to support their mission and their vision beyond padding your own pockets. As you further solidify your relationship with your customer through such actions, referrals come without asking.

- *Share valuable content.* This doesn't mean that you need to be an excellent writer. You just need to understand your customer well enough to know what information would be of value to them. Research articles that might pertain to their business and share with them, letting them know you were just thinking of them and wanted to share. Be fully engaged.

- *Say thank you.* Again, this seems obvious, but you'd be surprised how much this simple task is overlooked by many sales professionals. Your customers want to be appreciated and just saying thank you for their business goes a long way. Don't ever overlook the small things. When was the last time you wrote a handwritten thank you note and sent it to someone? While it might be old fashioned, it has become a lost art in our digital age. You'd be surprised how much your customer will appreciate a simple thank you note, letting them know how much you appreciate them and their business.

B.U.D. STRATEGY FOR NURTURING THE CUSTOMER

BETTER: Don't quit on your new customer once you earn their business. Continue to nurture and grow your relationship with them. They are waiting to see if you are going to follow through with what you told them you would do. Don't disappoint them.

UNIQUE: Go the extra mile. Be willing to do what others are not willing to do to show your customers that you appreciate them. A little bit goes a long way. Integrate your communication with your customers with your prospecting communication. It's just as important that you stay engaged with your customers as your prospects.

DESIRABLE: Be thankful for their business. Always take the time to show them how much you appreciate what they are doing for you. Create an experience that will not only make them happy with your business, but that will encourage them to share with their colleagues and friends.

CHAPTER 12: SALES MYTHS

Like everything, there are always myths in the world of sales, things that you think might be serving you well because someone told you it was the right thing to do, when in fact, that advice was holding you back.

This section of the book is designed to go over some sales myths that might have been holding you back in your sales success.

Myth: Technology alone will boost your sales.
Fact: Technology used correctly will dramatically improve your sales performance.

The mistake sales professionals make is relying too heavily on technology to produce results. Technology alone will never close the sale for you. Nothing will ever replace the human touch. Your customers and prospects still need to know that you care about them, and you cannot discern or convey emotion in an email or text message. That doesn't mean that technology doesn't have a place in sales, and it certainly doesn't mean that it won't help you improve your productivity and ability to close sales. When used as a tool to compliment what you do, it can be a tremendous asset. Don't, however, become too reliant upon it or use it as a crutch. Technology can never replace your ability to grow and sustain a relationship.

Myth: Chase every prospect until they break down and become your customer.
Fact: Be persistent, yet judicious.

You've probably been told to never give up on a prospect or let them slip from your fingers, even when the timing is not right. Sales does require patience and there will be customers that will take some time to grow and cultivate, but there will also be those who were never meant to be your customers in the first place. That's why it's so important to do your homework and know your customer avatar. Sometimes it's okay to let a prospect walk away because you genuinely are not a good fit for one another. One of the gems of this situation is you gain the respect of that person because you were authentic and didn't show yourself to be a desperate salesperson, willing to do anything to get the sale. Who knows? You might even gain a new friend from the encounter. You've heard of strategic partners, right? It's possible that a person who wasn't a good fit for you as a customer might take to you and decide someone else is and become a referral partner for you.

The other disadvantage of just throwing prospects at the wall and waiting to see what sticks is that it will eventually lead to burn out. It's not fun dealing with a lot of rejection, and while that is part of the process in sales, you are increasing your chance of rejection by not approaching qualified prospects. Don't you want to work smarter rather than harder?

Myth: The lowest price always wins.
Fact: Never get into the price game with a prospect.

You never want to get into a price war with your prospect or customer. Anytime that becomes the sole conversation between you and your prospect, you are fighting a losing battle. If it so happens that your product or service comes in lower than the competition, great, but you still don't want to focus on this. You always want to sell value to your prospect. Remind them of your unique selling proposition and why you are the best fit for them. Focus on their particular challenge and how you are going to solve it. If you want to talk numbers, break down how your solution will put dollars back into their pockets because of what it will give them back in time and productivity. Talk ROI (Return on Investment). This is a much more valuable conversation than discussing whose price is the highest or lowest.

Myth: You will close more sales by focusing on product features.
Fact: You will close sales by listening to the prospect and highlighting benefits.

You've heard this before - you always sell benefits over features. I don't care how many bells and whistles your product or service has; your prospect doesn't care. The only thing they care about is the fact that they have a problem, and they are talking to you to solve it. Features are not what solves their problems - not directly anyway. You want to speak directly to their pain points. Talk to them about what keeps them up at night and then discuss viable solutions to solve that problem. That is where your benefits come in. Share with them how your solution will benefit them directly and change their current situation. Once you get this, you have your prospect on the hook and they are ready to sign on the dotted line.

Myth: Say yes to everything.
Fact: No one can say yes to everything. Under promise and overdeliver.

It's commonplace in the sales world to hear about sales professionals that promise their prospects the world, only to end up disappointing them once they finally become customers. You don't want to be that salesperson. No one can say yes to everything - disappointment is waiting for you around every corner if you deploy that strategy. It is important to set appropriate expectations with your prospect, especially early in the relationship. It is tempting to want to tell your prospect that you can do everything that they ask for or want, but don't set yourself up for failure. Instead, under promise and overdeliver. If you're unsure if you can follow through on a request that they desire, be honest with them. If you are able to come through and fulfill that request for them later, you look like a rock star because you provided them with an unexpected surprise. Unexpected surprises are always better than disappointments any day of the week. No matter how tempting, don't say yes to everything. You can still close the sale, even when you have to say no.

Examine your own process to ensure you are not allowing any of these myths to hold you back in your sales progress. If any of this looks familiar to you, course correct and watch your productivity and sales start to climb.

B.U.D. STRATEGY FOR SALES MYTHS

BETTER: *Acknowledge whether or not you are letting a sales myth hold you back from success in your business and if so, adjust.*

UNIQUE: *Admit when you are wrong and need to make a change. It is easy to go with the flow and do what you do because that is what has always been done, or it's what* *everyone else is doing. However, if you discover your practices fall into one of these sales myths and it is affecting your sales, you owe it to yourself to change.*

DESIRABLE*: Part of growing as a professional is always seeking to grow. To do this, you must acknowledge when something that once worked isn't working anymore or if something you've become comfortable with isn't yielding you results. Small changes to improve and grow yourself will only make you a more desirable asset to your company and your customers.*

FINAL THOUGHTS

I hope you enjoyed this book and were able to learn some practical steps to apply in your sales career. Sales is quite a simple process. That doesn't make it easy, however. It requires diligence, a love of your craft and organization.

This book was designed to help you evaluate your own sales processes and techniques and identify areas to improve or omit. We never truly arrive. Even if you have been in sales for over 20 years, there is always something new to learn. If you remain humble throughout your career and always keep your mind open to learning and growing, you can be very successful.

If there is one filter I'd advise you to use throughout your daily sales tasks, it would be:

Am I Better?
Am I Unique?
Am I Desirable?

Filtering your activities through the B.U.D. process will most certainly ensure that you stay among the cream of the crop in the sales hemisphere.

BONUS CHAPTER: SALES EXCELLENCE

COMMUNICATION

Have you ever heard someone say, "you have a natural gift for sales"? While that is a compliment, the process to becoming a good sales professional requires the development of several different skill sets. Some of those skill sets may overlap with your natural abilities which is great, but some may require some work. The good news is that skills can be developed with practice. One of the most important skills for a successful sales professional is communication skills. Communication comes in many different formats including verbal, written, body language and even listening. Each of these play a vital role in facilitating a successful sale.

Verbal Communication
Verbal is the most obvious form of communication. It is how you communicate directly with your customer or prospect when you're asking questions or going over product benefits with them. Don't overdo verbal communication with your prospect. While it is important to be clear and explain to them the benefits of your product or service, you don't want to do a product dump on them. No prospect likes that. Your verbal communication should consist of an even exchange between you and your prospect. As matter of fact, the more verbal communication you receive from the prospect, the better because you cannot propose an ideal solution for them without learning more about them first.

Non-Verbal Communication

Non-verbal communication is just as important as verbal communication. Active listening is one of the most important skills a salesperson can learn in their career, and is often the skill most are quite deficient in. Take the time to really listen to your prospect. Learn about their business and their pain points. Listening actively means turning off all distractions, not interrupting them, and fully focusing on what they are telling you. There is nothing more annoying to a customer or prospect than to tell you everything they need and then have you follow that up by asking a question they just answered. That is not active listening. Confirm that you are listening to your prospect by following up with clarifying questions and repeating what they've told you. That assures them that you are, in fact, listening to them.

Body language is always a key indicator of how your prospect is responding to your direct communication. Ignoring these signals can easily result in the loss of a sale. Is your prospect making eye contact with you? Do they lean forward in anticipation of what you are about to tell them? These are signs that they are engaged. Or are they sitting back with their arms crossed? Are they refusing to make direct eye contact with you? Are they distracted, playing on their computer or their phone? These are indicators that you do not have your prospect's attention and that you are losing them fast. If you are not attentive to your prospect and looking for these signals, you will miss the chance to respond in kind. Conversely, your prospect is looking for the same body language from you. Do you stand upright and look them in the eye? This is a sign of confidence. Slouching and lack of eye contact communicates to the prospect that you are unprofessional and unsure of yourself. Skills can be developed with practice.

Written Communication

Written communication does not play a large role while you are meeting with your prospect, but it is vital when you are in the process of setting up a meeting and following up. How clear and concise is your communication? Does it reflect that you take an active interest in their needs? Does it have typos? These are all important aspects to consider when communicating with your prospect because a bad impression can mean a lost opportunity. Learn how to master the art of communication. It will not only help you develop into a great sales professional, but you will find that it will help with your own personal relationships as well.

THE HUMAN TOUCH

Contrary to popular belief, good sales professionals are heartfelt individuals that genuinely care about people. A lot of people associate sales with a negative stigma, the used car salesperson who will try to sell you everything you don't need to achieve his own agenda. Don't get me wrong – those types of salespeople do exist, but they are not your most successful salespeople. Successful sales professionals are relatable, outwardly revealing to their prospects their human side.

Empathy

Because good sales professionals solve problems, they are also empathetic to the problems their prospects experience. They care. It is difficult to build relationships and connect with your prospects or customers if you are cold hearted. Prospects can sense when a salesperson is genuinely interested in what they have to say and when they are just giving lip service to try and land the sale.

Personable

A good sales professional needs to have a personality. Don't get into a career where you have to deal with people if you are not a people person. Sales requires great people skills because you have to interface with customers, prospects and your internal office staff on a regular basis. You are often the liaison between the client and the company once you establish an account; therefore, it's important that you know how to handle different personalities and learn how to relate to each. Good sales professionals can also manage conflict with a customer or prospect just as easily as they handle praise. Adaptable: Sales professionals have to navigate change on a regular basis. Each customer or prospect has different needs and none of them fit nicely into a little box. As a sales professional, you have to learn to adapt to the different needs of the customers you serve. No one day is alike because no customer is alike. They all have different needs, and you must be ready and willing to rise to the occasion to meet those needs.

Fearless

Sales professionals face rejection on daily basis. It's not always easy to pick up the phone and make another cold call after receiving that rejection, but it is a necessary step to get that one person who will say yes and take a meeting. It's a numbers game and the sooner you learn not to take anything personal and just move forward, the easier it will become.

The bottom line is good sales professionals are human just like you. They care about people and simply want to work with their customers to make their lives easier. While many make great income, they are not all about the dollar bill. Good sale professionals genuinely care about people.

B.U.D. STRATEGY FOR SALES EXCELLENCE

BETTER: Communication is verbal, nonverbal, and written. Leverage all methods of communication to be responsive to your client's needs.

UNIQUE: Listening is necessary skill for sales professionals. A common error is already knowing what you're going to tell your client before you've heard what they have to say. You should certainly have some ideas ahead of time, but it's important to spend time planning the questions you will ask your client or prospect. Then show them you are listening with your communication skills.

DESIRABLE: We're often taught that to be 'professional' we shouldn't show our personality. This limits the relationships you can build with your clients. Get to know your clients personally and let them get to know you. People choose to work with professionals they can trust. You can keep it professional and still be yourself.

BONUS CASE STUDIES

MOSHE

Moshe started his business in 2013 and everything seemed to be going well until he reached a plateau in acquiring new customers. I connected with Moshe at a networking event several years after he'd opened his business. After connecting with Moshe and learning more about his challenges, we decided to work together.

Our primary focus was using social media as a tool to help him prospect and grow business. Moshe learned how to be proactive and confident without being pushy. I taught him that every prospect is not a good fit for his business. We worked on identifying what his ideal customer looked like and tailoring his prospecting process accordingly.

Moshe's confidence grew in his ability to network and use social media to nurture relationships and grow his business. This was a big achievement for him because he'd struggled with this before.

After our work together, Moshe learned:

- How to engage and get more results
- How to unlock his ability to be more proactive in his business
- How to be more bold (without being pushy)
- How to approach confrontation and opportunities without running away from them

MARVIN

Marvin took one of my LinkedIn training courses initially. When we met, he was just starting his consulting practice. We decided to work together, starting with identifying specific sales strategies he should put in place.

First, we had to identify his customer avatar. Once we understood who his customer was, we could get more focused on meeting their specific needs. From there, we could guide the customer through the sales process and build value.

The next step was teaching Marvin how to build relationships and nurture through digital strategies, with a particular focus on LinkedIn.

Through our work together, Marvin was able to grow his LinkedIn connections to over 500 within one month. He continued to make business contacts and grew his network. Through this process, Marvin gained clarity on the sales funnel lens.

Marvin says he continues to use the strategies I taught him in his business today. He learned to build business by helping and solving problems, not focusing on the sale. He is more customer focused and has learned to be purpose driven in his sales.

AFTERWORD

It's at this point in the book where we separate the readers from the doers. Readers, the larger group of the two, will put down the book, note some actions, soak in the validation for techniques and concepts already used, and move on. Doers will set out to understand and deploy what they learned and the put it into practice. The great news is that if you are reading this section, you are more likely a doer than a reader, and are thus ready to implement. Fantastic! Do you know why? Because everything you need to succeed is present, including you.

Most sales books will give readers the 'what' and the 'why' of things. These are easy to present, but harder to measure. While you feel good reading, it is missing the key ingredient, the 'how'. It is a fact that this book, at every turn, focuses on the 'how'. The core concept introduced early, B.U.D., is easy to remember and apply; you just have to follow the breadcrumbs. In each chapter, we are introduced to specific concepts, why the concepts are important, and specific related actions, allowing you to try, adapt, and refine.

The most wonderful thing about this book, is that it is an example of the principles to which it speaks: being better prepared; unique in having a plan; desirable in how it simplifies sales concepts rather than over complicating.

One subject of interest in the book is the examination of excuses. Every salesperson has either excuses or execution. Again, if you got this far, I am betting what got you here was the curiosity and appetite for more. One more nugget you can apply to your sales process, one more way to engage with potential buyers. Which is why the book delivers: it includes the 'how', tied to specific 'why's.

As the author explores different elements of the sales process, he neatly ties it back to the nucleus of the book, B.U.D. Better – Unique – Desirable. This allows you, the reader, to layer in the core concepts without upending your current approach. You can evolve rather than be jolted into change and growth.

The ultimate quality of this book is the lack of pretense that one finds in many sales books. Instead it focuses on the fundamentals, absent of the philosophy lessons that accompany some sales advice. The focus is on execution, and success in sales is all about execution. Everything else is just talk!

Tibor Shanto
Chief Prospecting Officer
Renbor Sales Solutions Inc.

ABOUT THE AUTHOR

Thomas Ellis is sales management veteran with over 30 years' experience in coaching, consulting, and developing sales personnel and managers. Thomas began his professional sales career in the copier industry and then moved to the telecommunications industry, where he was employed by Motorola and Nextel (which merged with Sprint in 2005). Thomas spent 13 years with Sprint Nextel where he held several Sales Manager and Director of Sales positions. He received Sprint/Nextel's highest sales award, President's Council for 10 consecutive years.

Thomas is considered by many to be a subject matter expert (SME) in coaching and developing business-to-business sales professionals. Thomas is highly regarded as the Expert "Sales 101" Trainer. During his tenure at Sprint/Nextel, he developed and coached sales representatives and sales managers that had clients from small- to medium-businesses, enterprises, education markets, state and local government, and the federal government.

Currently Thomas is the President and Chief Sales Coach for EWC Consultants where he works with small business owners and sales professionals on mastering easy and simple sales strategies that help them close big deals.

In this role, Thomas has coached and advised hundreds of small business owners, sales leaders, and sales professionals in a wide range of industries helping them to win more business. He has written several ebooks on sales, and he frequently facilitates workshops to help small business owners and sales professionals master the basic tenets of sales. He believes that if you master the basics of the selling process that you will be wildly successful.

Thomas was educated at Fordham University in New York City where he received a Bachelor of Science degree in Business Administration. When he is not working, Thomas enjoys playing golf, mentoring young adults, and spending time with his grandchildren.

Reach out to Thomas:

www.tellissalescoach.com
www.linkedin.com/in/thomaseellis
tellissalescoach@outlook.com
301-343-0001

REVIEWS

"Fabulous book for those of us that have had a career in sales as well as for those just starting out. Thomas is the ultimate 'Sales 101' teacher! His B.U.D. (Better, Unique & Desirable) technique is applicable to every step of the sales process and to all sales situations. His writing style is easy and relatable. This book is a 'basics' reminder for experienced sales professionals and a terrific guide for beginners. I highly recommend this book! Easy read and very informational!"

- Joe Alvarez, Principal, NOS – National Office Systems

"Thomas uses the framework of 'Better, Unique, and Desirable' throughout the sales process to illustrate how to get on the same side with your clients and prospects to achieve results."

- Ian Altman, Bestselling Co-author, *Same Side Selling*

"The B.U.D. approach is an easy to understand and apply strategy to help new and seasoned sales professionals improve their performance and achieve new heights in their sales career. Thomas clearly shows how you can apply these proven techniques to differentiate yourself from the competition and earn the trust and respect of both prospects and clients. I highly recommend this book to sales professionals and sales leaders wanting to achieve better results."

- Vincent Burruano, Vice President Sales, Commercial Services Division, JK Moving Services

"In his book, *B.U.D. Better, Unique, & Desirable: The Sales Process That Gets Results*, Thomas Ellis provides salespeople with a road map for success in the information age. He clearly outlines the sales process that should be followed for communicating value, helping customers with their buying decision, and building long-term and worthwhile relationships. Thomas supports his work with useful case studies, and he communicates his expertise in bite-sized nuggets of easy-to-understand knowledge with a clear call to action. As a senior sales leader of leaders, I highly recommend Thomas's book for anyone who wants to better connect with their customers in a more meaningful way and drive more topline revenue."

- Bob Greene, CEO, RCG Workgroup

"I agree with so much of this... 'You are not the used car salesperson'! Thomas Ellis's book is filled with so many easy-to-digest and internalize nuggets of sales tips. Definitely a must read for the sales professional at every stage of development. B.U.D. serves as an instructional for the novice, a refresher to the seasoned salesperson, and a reference tool for the sales manager."

- Dennis Harris, Senior Managing Partner, SURE, LLC

"*B.U.D. Better, Unique, & Desirable: The Sales Process That Gets Results* explores several counterintuitive routes to sales success, but it starts with the most important skill of all: preparation. If we want to impress others—with our ideas, our products, our services, or even ourselves—we have to conduct research and understand to whom we are talking. And if you listen to Thomas Ellis, you'll learn the attitudes and abilities required to master the new world of sales."

- Patrick McFadden, Founder & Marketing Consultant, Indispensable Marketing

"There are few books on sales and sales process that inspire a vetted sales veteran to take notes and highlight key themes throughout the book for themselves and their clients; however, that is exactly what I found myself doing as I read, *B.U.D. Better, Unique, & Desirable: The Sales Process That Gets Results*. Thomas does an incredible job of simplifying the process and providing bite-sized nuggets for the reader to consume, then apply to make themselves a B.U.D. sales professional. Whether you are new to sales or leading a multi-national team, this is the new roadmap to winning in sales!"

- Ed Ross, Global Sales Enablement Consultant

"Thomas Ellis is B.U.D. From the moment I met him, I was drawn to his ability to make selling more interesting and engaging to prospects. His process is easy to follow and gets results. This book is engaging and full of relatable stories around mindset, networking, building relationships, prospecting, running appointments properly, moving sales forward, closing business, and nurturing clients. Each of these golden nuggets are positioned to help sales professionals serve their client more effectively by selling better. Two thumbs up. A must read for anyone looking to improve their sales process."

- Brynne Tillman, CEO, LinkedIn Whisperer at Social Sales Link

REFERENCES

Brudner, E. (2018, July 23). *9 little-known ways to find new prospects on LinkedIn.* HubSpot. Retrieved from: https://blog.hubspot.com/sales/little-known-ways-to-find-new-prospects-on-linkedin

Merriam-Webster. (n.d.) *Essential Meaning of Passion.* Retrieved Dec. 10, 2021, from: https://www.merriam-webster.com/dictionary/passion

Stec, C. (2021, July 30). *14 effective ways to get high-quality referrals from your customers.* HubSpot. Retrieved from: https://blog.hubspot.com/service/how-to-get-referrals

Thomas, A. (2019, October 31). *5 sales myths I learned while closing tens of millions in revenue.* Inc.com. Retrieved from: https://www.inc.com/andrew-thomas/5-big-sales-myths-i-learned-while-closing-tens-of-millions-in-revenue.html

Made in the USA
Coppell, TX
17 February 2022

73721035R00079